Leonardo DiCaprio

An Intimate Portrait

Colin MacLean

ICON PRESS

© 2004 by Folklore Publishing
First printed in 2004 10 9 8 7 6 5 4 3 2 1
Printed in Canada

All rights reserved. No part of this work covered by the copyrights hereon may be reproduced or used in any form or by any means—graphic, electronic or mechanical—without the prior written permission of the publisher, except for reviewers, who may quote brief passages. Any request for photocopying, recording, taping or storage on information retrieval systems of any part of this work shall be directed in writing to the publisher.

The Publisher: Icon Press, an imprint of Folklore Publishing

Website: www.folklorepublishing.com

Library and Archives Canada Cataloguing in Publication

MacLean, Colin, 1936–
 Leonardo DiCaprio : an intimate portrait / Colin MacLean.

(Star biographies)
Includes bibliographical references.
ISBN 1-894864-21-2

 1. DiCaprio, Leonardo. 2. Motion picture actors and actresses—United States—Biography. I. Title. II. Series.

PN2287.D453M32 2005   791.4302'8'092   C2004-907061-4

Project Director: Faye Boer
Editorial: Faye Boer, Nicholle Carrière
Layout & Production: Trina Koscielnuk
Cover Design: Valentino
Book Design: Anne & Dion

Cover Image: Courtesy of International Communications Systems

Photography credits: Every effort has been made to accurately credit the sources of photographs. Any errors or omissions should be directed to the publisher for changes in future editions. Photographs courtesy of International Communications Systems.

We acknowledge the support of the Alberta Foundation for the Arts for our publishing program.

PC:P6

Table of Contents

Dedication 3
Introduction 4

Chapter 1 8
Chapter 2 16
Chapter 3 24
Chapter 4 34
Chapter 5 42
Chapter 6 50
Chapter 7 62
Chapter 8 72
Chapter 9 82
Chapter 10 94
Chapter 11 100
Chapter 12 112
Chapter 13 122
Chapter 14 130

Filmography 140
Notes on Sources 142

Dedication

To Halia, who sat through a lifetime of movies with patience and love while I searched for life at 24 f/s.

Introduction

The earliest memories I have are of going to the movies. The era of the great cinema palaces was just ending, but there were still enough of them around to remind a small patron with ticket in sweaty hand that he was about to embark on a grand adventure. Ushers in round beanie hats and uniforms stood ready to guide you to the loges up the long marble staircases covered with a sumptuous red carpet. Inside, angels danced on a cloud-covered ceiling lit by a huge crystal chandelier. And they had such impressive names evocative of an even grander time—the Tivoli, the Strand, the Regent.

> Ushers in round beanie hats and uniforms stood ready to guide you to the loges up the long marble staircases covered with a sumptuous red carpet.

Even today when the curtain raises in a small art movie house or a large cineplex, the thrill and sense of adventure of those formative years remains.

The dream of being part of the movies never left me even as I pursued a career in radio and television. In the early '80s, I designed a format for movie reviews that would fit, like a module, into any newscast. It worked, and in a short time, I found myself syndicated to television stations all over the country.

About six months later the phone rang and a voice said, "Hi, this is Paramount Pictures. Would you like to fly to Hollywood to interview John Travolta and Jamie Lee Curtis for their new film *Perfect*?

Would I!

And thus began my life as a Hollywood junketeer. During the next 15 years I spent much of my time flying across the world to interview moviemakers about their creations. I talked to Steve Martin, Lassie (yes, the Collie,

with her handler) and Tom Cruise on set of their latest films. I met Michael Caine in London and Nick Nolte in North Carolina. I attended world premieres with the Coen brothers, Vin Diesel and Kevin Costner. But mostly I flew to New York and Los Angeles where the players were ensconced in five-star hotels, and I interviewed them about their lives and films. Although our talks were mostly short, I often had the opportunity to push beyond the usual questions about a star's latest release. Yes, Steven Spielberg loves to talk movies. When you can get through the armies of hard-nosed, prickly handlers that constantly surround him, Tom Cruise has enough charm to sell icebergs to Inuit. Robert De Niro, that most intelligent of movie actors, has problems stringing together coherent sentences in interviews.

> **You will read more about this singular exercise in movie tinsel and glitz (and wearying physical demand) in the following pages. And through it all, the movies never the lost the magic that enveloped the small boy in the fabulously ornate movie houses of yore. Moviemakers still spin glorious tales that stir our imagination and haunt our dreams. And it should come as no surprise to anyone who goes to the cinema that movie stars just aren't like you and I.**

 I guess that's why they are movie stars.

In this book, you will meet one of the most interesting and complex of the current gods of the silver screen. Perhaps Leonard DiCaprio's story is not unique. He travels down an often dark and rocky road with few signs to guide him—a road well trodden by movie stars before him. He has stumbled, picked himself up and then gone on to become the face that defines the movies for a new generation of filmgoers.

An actor, yes. A larger-than-life personality adored by audiences of both sexes—that too. His life is both outrageous and ordinary. Like Valentino, Gable and Dean before him, he is a movie star.

I hope you'll enjoy meeting him.

chapter 1

"Is the day so young"

—Romeo (Leonardo DiCaprio) to Juliet (Clair Danes)
in William Shakespeare's *Romeo + Juliet*.

Leonardo DiCaprio is not happy.

For the better part of a day, he's been standing in a ship's cabin that is repeatedly being filled with freezing water. The cabin is tilting at an awkward angle making it difficult to maintain his footing. He is attached to a pipe, giving him little room to move. Just inches from the end of his chiseled nose is a huge Panavision camera sitting on the shoulder of producer/writer/director James Cameron. The obsessive director is demanding his usual "one more shot," while his crew scrambles to reset the scene.

The actor, like the crew, is ready to give Cameron whatever he wants. The director, whose short fuse is legendary, is already growling at his crew. After each film Cameron makes, many of his team grumble that they will never work with the man again. This shoot has already been so arduous that some have stormed out. But they always come back. Making a film with James Cameron becomes an exhausting quest following one man's near-fanatical vision, and everyone involved gets caught up in his fevered dream knowing no one will work harder and longer than the director.

> Making a film with James Cameron becomes an exhausting quest following one man's near-fanatical vision, and everyone involved gets caught up in his fevered dream...

The cameras roll, and DiCaprio becomes adventurer Jack Dawson, shackled to a pipe and unable to escape while the contents of the room float around him. He watches in growing horror as the tiny cabin fills with water. In another shot but at the same time, the prow of the *Titanic* begins its slow slide into the dark North Atlantic.

This might have been a good time for DiCaprio to reconsider why he took the job in the first place. He really wasn't interested in playing the lead in Cameron's epic take on the sinking of the *Titanic*. The rising young star had come to think of himself as a character actor like his heroes Johnny Depp, Benicio Del Toro and Robert De Niro. From *Romeo + Juliet* to *What's Eating Gilbert Grape*, he had made his reputation playing maladjusted misfits, and the actor wasn't sure he wanted to play a romantic hero.

> Cameron wasn't convinced either. He was under pressure from the studio to use the currently hot Matthew McConaughey. "The curious thing is that I actually didn't want Leo at first. Leo was recommended by the studios, as were other hot, young actors. He didn't strike me as necessarily having the qualities I wanted in Jack. But I met him and basically loved him. He can charm a group of people without doing anything obvious. The second I met him I was convinced."

As he had many times before in his professional career, DiCaprio almost sabotaged his own audition. He found to his surprise that he liked the character Cameron had invented for him. As he later remembered in a cozy New York hotel room just before the release of the film and months after he had dried out from the experience, "I was interested because I've traditionally played characters that have been tortured in some aspect, whether it be by love or drugs or whatever. But this guy was like an open book. He was an openhearted guy with no demons, and it was more of a challenge than I ever thought it would be. I would like to be like that character. I mean, Jack just sort of embodies a lot of things that I think we all find admirable. Like a Bohemian that lives day to day finds his own sort of happiness. You try to be like that. I wish…I think I do have some of those aspects, but he's almost like the kind of guy we all wish to be."

Despite that, DiCaprio couldn't help himself during the audition. "He read it once and then started goofing around," Cameron remembers ruefully. But in the moment that DiCaprio gave him, Cameron saw the Jack he wanted and later, in the first of many intimate one-on-one conversations director and star were to have in the months ahead, they struck a deal. DiCaprio agreed to go along with the Cameron's vision.

"I'm not going to make this guy brooding and neurotic. I'm not going to give him a tic or a limp," insisted Cameron. The director wanted a straight, accessible and hugely likeable romantic hero. So DiCaprio became the Jack Dawson we saw on that big screen, and when he was not happy with his dialogue, he was still capable of engaging in some heated discussion with the director. For example, Leonardo hated the "king of the world" line. He considered it too smarmy. He lost that battle, and it became an internationally known catchphrase

> But in the moment that DiCaprio gave him, Cameron saw the Jack he wanted and later, in the first of many intimate one-on-one conversations director and star were to have in the months ahead, they struck a deal.

as well as the well-remembered quote in James Cameron's Oscar acceptance speech.

> **DiCaprio also knew that the role carried with it the star stature that would give him additional clout in Hollywood and a wider choice of roles in the future. It would also be his first check for over $1 million.**

The camera loved Leonardo DiCaprio from his first appearance as a child actor. Directors of photography have often noted that he doesn't seem to have a bad angle and looks great in any light. His friend Mark Wahlberg, a remarkably handsome young hunk himself, once observed, "He has the bad luck of being prettier than most of the actresses in his movies." "He is simply a beautiful man and a wonderful person," gushes his *Titanic* co-star Kate Winslet. When asked about Leonardo's well-documented and prodigious ability to party to all hours, she laughs, "He'd walk onto the set in the morning, and after an hour's sleep, and that face…it took your breath away. I'd just looked at him, having been through hours of make-up for myself and wailed, 'You rotter.' He practically rolled out of bed and looked gorgeous."

When you first meet Leonardo DiCaprio you notice that he is tall and a bit gangly (and if you saw *The Beach*, that he has skinny legs). At nearly 6 feet tall, he weighs in at only about 140 pounds (unless he has bulked up for a role). With his startling blue green eyes and (again depending on the role) a mop of darkish blond hair, his presence in a room is riveting. He is bright, energetic, fun-loving, sexy, charming, articulate and

> **Because of those demonstrable acting abilities built up over a series of acclaimed roles and a wide variety of films, top directors want to work with him.**

charismatic. He is sometimes moody and has difficulty disguising his dislike of the press.

Far more than just another pretty face, he has shown remarkable range in his choice of roles. He can look back at a career that in just a decade has already brilliantly blended commercial success with artistic acclaim. He has also made a few clunkers along the way. He is a man with a huge appetite for life, observing with a twinkle, "I've always been wild. Now I have a lot more material to work with."

> He began his professional life doing commercials for everything from MatchBox cars to bubble gum and has risen to the top of his profession.

Despite the gusher that was *Titanic*, Leonardo has managed to keep his life moored to what he feels is important. As he moved beyond the image of the teen hunk that electrified much of the world in *Titanic*, he has become a mature actor currently at the top of his game. His past co-stars all speak highly of him and value the time they spent together. "He is just so normal and fundamental," exudes Winslet. "He's very chatty and so funny that we laughed and joked around all the time. He's great." After working with him in Steven Spielberg's *Catch Me If You Can*, Toms Hanks enthused, "Leo is the hardest working, most intelligent actor I've ever come across." Because of those demonstrable acting abilities built up over a series of acclaimed roles and a wide variety of films, top directors want to work with him. "He is the best young actor working in films today," said Martin Scorsese quoted in the *Dallas Morning News*. "The best thing about acting," Leonardo, the one-time class clown, observed, "is that I get to lose myself in another character and actually get paid for it. As for myself, I'm not sure who I am. It seems to change every day."

Leonardo learned by doing—he has never taken an acting lesson.

> His reaction to comment on his physical charms is, "When I look into the mirror, I don't see beauty. I see an insecure actor who has spent most of his life wondering where his next job is going to come from." He added to that remark on television's ***Good Morning America*** when he noted, "There's always a new pretty face. You definitely want to be remembered for your work rather than being the hunk-of-the-month deal. That's what I've always aimed for."

Leonardo, who has interviewed presidents and written for *Time* magazine on the subject, is vitally interested in the environment, especially animals that are threatened by extinction. His official website is packed with information about the great apes and other endangered species, as well as warnings about biodiversity and the fragility of the world's oceans. The site also urges his young fans to get out and vote and provides the latest information on global warming. He has been known to grab a reporter's tape machine and give long, impassioned monologues on environmental issues. He supports AIDS research, helps the homeless and the Make-A-Wish Foundation, which grants wishes to children with life-threatening illnesses. In his hometown of Los Feliz (a part of Greater Los Angeles), his family paid for the construction of a high-tech computer and multimedia center at the local library. The Leonardo DiCaprio Computer Center opened in June 1999 and stands in the spot where Leo's childhood house once stood.

The actor's choices for roles have often been dark, quirky and offbeat and have taken him down some challenging and often unexpected roads. Much of what he is today was forged by an unusual childhood filled with exuberance, freedom and a singular lack of parental restriction, leaving him with rich memories. His integrity, convictions, perspectives and drive can be traced to his childhood and his remarkable relationship with his parents and friends.

chapter 2

When you got **nuthin'**, you got **nuthin'** to lose.

—Jack Dawson (Leonardo DiCaprio), in a card game just before winning the fateful ticket in *Titanic*.

The story sounds like the creation of some overachieving Hollywood hack, but it has moved into the mythic lore of the Leonardo DiCaprio canon so it's worth repeating.

Leo's mother, Irmalin Idenbirken, is a pretty blonde woman born in Germany. His father, George DiCaprio, was an underground comic artist whose life was (and is) unconventional and nonconformist. The two met in college in New York, fell in love and were married. One day in 1974, the couple was walking through the Uffizi Museum in Florence, Italy, where they were drawn to a work by Leonardo da Vinci. As they were standing there marveling at what they saw, the expectant mother felt a particularly sharp kick from the child she was carrying. Irmalin decided that it was some sort of sign and that her unborn child would bear the name of the great Italian Renaissance painter and visionary.

On November 11 of that year, Leonardo Wilhelm DiCaprio was born in Los Angeles. The DiCaprios, like so many before them, had moved to L.A. because they felt that it was the city of dreams and opportunity. But what they found was just the opposite. Money was scarce for the small family, so they moved into the rundown Garfield Apartments just north of Hollywood Boulevard. George eked out a meager living distributing underground comic books from his garage to newsstands and avant-garde bookstores. He also arranged readings for controversial writers and poets such as William S. Burroughs and Allen Ginsberg.

The financial pressures soon proved too much for the relationship, and George and

Irmalin split up. The two remained close friends as Leo and his mother moved to a small but sunshine-filled home in the Los Feliz section of the city, not far from where his father lived with Leo's new stepmother, Peggy. Living apart or not, the DiCaprios decided they would provide a warm and supportive life for their child.

The neighborhood young Leo grew up in was a seedy world of prostitutes, massage parlors and drug users—not the best kind of place to raise a curious, active child. But like many children raised in such circumstances, it was all the boy knew. And although he was aware of the pain and harsh realities that surrounded him, he remembers his life during those years as an adventure. At night, the neighborhood came alive with sirens, fights and street-corner sex for sale. "It was crazy back then," says his father. "Kind of a red-light district." Charles Bukowski, the alcoholic alternative poet, whose life was the subject of the movie *Barfly*, lived just across the street from Leo's father and became a close friend of George and his inquisitive young son.

> **George's house was a welcoming place where all kinds of musicians, artists, authors as well as those from the fringes of society gathered. Underground comic artists such as Robert Crumb and Harvey Pekar were frequent guests, as was political radical Abbie Hoffman's son, America, who became one of Leo's closest friends.**

It's no wonder that young Leo grew up with an interest in many things. Broken home or not, his solid relationship with both parents generated a spirit of security and love that gave him a solid, positive grounding. They didn't have much money, so they lavished love and attention on their child, ensuring that he could express his creative side. They took him to museums, poetry readings, parades and street festivals. The local schools weren't up to the educational standard the DiCaprios wanted for their son, so every day his mother took an hour drove him an hour to a private elementary school in posh Westwood, and his father picked him up.

> "I hung out with a lot of kids that had much more money than we did. I got to hang out at some really fantastic homes, so while I didn't grow up with a lot of money, I grew up with that background. I was always treated in the best kind of way. My mother always wanted to give me the best," muses the actor. Irmalin was also one of Leo's best friends. He lived with her in a modest two-bedroom home until he moved into his own house in 1997, long after he had become a major star.

Leo was an outgoing, friendly young man, and people liked just being around him. He was creative and curious. Even as a child, just for fun, he would act out small scenes dressed up as various characters and entertain everyone around him. "I always wanted to be an actor," he remembers. "My parents knew I was an outgoing child, and whenever people came over, I'd automatically do impressions of them after they left. It was my mom's favorite thing." He was a polite, beautiful child with long, silky blond hair cut in a Prince Valiant style.

> He was creative and curious. Even as a child, just for fun, he would act out small scenes dressed up as various characters and entertain everyone around him.

Looking back, you could say that young Leo had a zest for life, but in those years, that sometimes translated into a kind of hyperactivity that made him difficult to control. At the age of five, he became fascinated by the children's television program *Romper Room*. Always on the lookout for something to keep Leo challenged and interested, his mother took him to the set and persuaded the producers to make him part of the cast. The people who guided the show were attracted to his natural good looks, and they went for the idea. But Leo turned out to be a small tornado in the studio. He would run up and smack the cameras, dash around the studio performing somersaults and flips and generally create havoc. He was eventually ejected from the show for "uncontrollable behavior," and it was many years before he appeared in front of a camera again.

George and Irmalin remained supportive, and in later years, Leo observed ruefully that he never had a rebellious youth because he had nothing to rebel against. His parents and stepmother never excluded their child from any conversation with their colorful friends—conversations that included everything from politics to sex and drugs. While other parents living in the neighborhood kept their children close and on tightly planned schedules, Leo was free to roam and take in new experiences wherever he found them.

Like most children, Leo developed a love for animals. He always had a pet cat or dog. He even went out hunting for frogs in a local swamp and brought home two of the homely creatures as pets. Not quite understanding the relationship between froggie life and the need for oxygen, he put them into a bowl while cleaning out their cage and covered the bowl tightly with plastic wrap so they couldn't hop out. When he returned to put them back in their home, both amphibians had expired.

Leo loved fishing with his parents off the coast of California. He grew so fond of life on the water that, for a time, he seriously considered becoming an

> His parents and stepmother never excluded their child from any conversation with their colorful friends—conversations that included everything from politics to sex and drugs.

oceanographer. As he grew older, he often talked of the world's exotic animals and endangered species. Of course, his career has taken him down a much different path, but he has become a strong spokesperson for the environment.

> Leo grew up alongside his older stepbrother Adam Starr, son of George's second wife. In fact, it was Adam's success that pushed Leo onto the yellow brick road to stardom. Adam was cast in a Golden Grahams breakfast cereal commercial. "I asked my dad how much Adam made from it," remembers Leo. "He said, 'About $50,000.'" "How cool is that," Leo thought and began to pressure his parents to come up with something for him. The pressure only increased when Adam landed a continuing role on the series **Battlestar Galactica**.

Irmalin had a friend who worked at a talent agency and got Leo an audition. He must have impressed the agents because he was soon on the audition circuit and suffering the reality of constant rejection. It must have been tough on the youngster because of the inevitable feeling that you are rejected because of something lacking in yourself, not because you are too old, too young or maybe your hair isn't just right. When he was 10, a casting agent rushed through a room full of children pointing and briskly declaring, "Not him. Not him. Maybe him. Not him." When she momentarily singled out the young DiCaprio and uttered the damning words "not him" before moving quickly on, Leo was crushed. "I went up to her and asked why she didn't pick me." "Wrong haircut," was the brusque reply. The embryonic actor was in tears on the way home. Between sobs he ground out, "Dad, I really want to become an actor, but if this is what it's

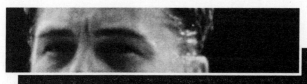

LEO FAN FACT

As a youth, Leonardo was nicknamed "Leonardo retardo" because of his often-outrageous behavior. He got through school (he says) by copying off his classmates' papers.

about, I don't want to do it." His dad put his arm around Leonardo and said, "Someday, Leo, it will happen for you. Just remember these words." Leo said, "Okay, Dad," and stopped crying.

They tried to get him to change his name. "Leonardo DiCaprio. Too ethnic," proclaimed one agent. "They wanted to change me into white bread," says Leo. "They wanted to fix it so I could go to auditions and say, 'Look, I'm Lenny Williams, and I have blond hair.'"

Leo kept his name and went back to the audition mill.

But slowly, his father's words spoken to a dejected child one afternoon following a failed audition proved prophetic. Leonardo was an attractive adolescent with a smile that could melt icebergs let alone a casting director's cold heart. Leo looked younger than his age, which was an advantage when it came to memorizing words and following directions. Four years later, he was featured in a commercial for MatchBox toy cars and trucks. Other spots for cereal and bubble gum followed. In all, between the ages of 14 and 16, he appeared in about 30 commercials. He was also offered real acting parts in longer productions—two educational films: *Mickey's Safety Club* and *How to Deal With a Parent Who Takes Drugs*.

Despite the openness of his face and friendly demeanor, producers detected hints of darkness. His return to series television was as a troubled teen in two episodes of *The New Adventures of Lassie*. Impressed, the producers of another short-lived series based on the Francis Ford Coppola film, *The Outsiders*, cast him in a similar role. He appeared on *Roseanne* and landed a continuing role as a teen alcoholic on the soap opera *Santa Barbara*.

He was 15.

> It looked as if the success he had yearned for as a boy was beginning to happen. Even then however, Leo was wise enough to see these roles as a broadening experience and a steppingstone to something bigger. As he told a reporter in 1990, "I hadn't played a cheerful boy yet. But playing emotionally ill characters gave me a chance to really act."

Leonardo may have enjoyed the challenge of playing a teenage drunk, but working in a soap opera isn't much fun, especially for a fun-loving 15 year old. The law only allowed him to work half-days, but he still had huge amounts of dialogue to learn. Leonardo was a bright young man but something of a slacker who never enjoyed school much, finding that the institution confined his restless spirit. On the set, he was tutored between scenes while still attending John Marshall High School. He observed years later, "I was frustrated in school. I know it's up to you to a degree, but a lot of times school is just so dull and boring. It's hard for a kid to learn in that environment. You go to school, you go to this class, study that, get your homework, go home. There is hardly any

> I had this science class where the teacher would give me 10 minutes after the class ended, and I would get up and do improv.

vibrancy there. I could never focus on things I didn't want to learn. I used to do break-dancing skits with my friend at lunchtime. I had this science class where the teacher would give me 10 minutes after the class ended, and I would get up and do improv. I needed to go to a place where I was excited about what I was learning. For me, it's all about getting a person interested in a subject by linking a lot of happiness to it—a lot of joy in doing it. That was lacking for me and maybe for a lot of other kids in the country."

Leonardo was the class clown and a disruption to his teachers. One day for a joke, he drew a swastika on his forehead as part of an improvisation about mass murderers. His teachers didn't get it and reported the incident to Leo's parents, who in typical fashion shrugged it off. He never did graduate with his class but instead received a GED—graduate equivalency diploma.

After a few months on the soap opera, he moved on. But his life and his career was about to ratchet up another notch, moving towards a looming iceberg, a doomed ship and a place as the best-known actor in the world.

chapter 3

Holy Saint Francis, what a change is here.

—Friar Lawrence (Peter Postlethwaite) to Romeo (Leonardo DiCaprio) in William Shakespeare's Romeo + Juliet

He may have found it tough slogging in school, but Leonardo's acting career was soaring. He loved doing the Ron Howard-directed movie *Parenthood*. The film, starring Steve Martin, was released in 1989 and became a $100-million hit at the box office. Leonardo was excited when he was asked to audition for the ensemble cast for the television series that followed. He gave the audition his best shot. "I knew what the character was like, and I knew I'd be good at it. I tried out for it, and then I went on callback. I was one of the final three. I really concentrated. I was in there and did my best, and I got the part."

Unfortunately, the audience that made the movie a huge success at the box office didn't support the television series, and it was cancelled after only 13 weeks. But as yet another troubled teen, Gary Buckman, Leonardo was not only sharpening his skills, he was attracting the attention of the power elite of Hollywood. With a regular weekly series on prime time, teenagers began to regard him as a hot new presence, and his picture began to appear in fan magazines with more frequency.

For seven years, *Growing Pains*, starring teen idol Kirk Cameron, racked up high ratings and an enthusiastic following. It was the story of Long Island psychiatrist, Jason Seaver (played by Alan Thicke), who

> "I knew what the character was like, and I knew I'd be good at it. I tried out for it, and then I went on callback. I was one of the final three."

Growing Pains (1991–92)

conducted his practice from his home, which included his wife and four children. By its seventh season, the series was growing tired, and Cameron was no longer hitting the target teen audience. So the producers looked for a new element to pump some life back into the faltering show. They hit upon the then 16-year-old Leonardo as a character who could lure back the fading teen audience. Leo played Luke Bower, a homeless boy who came to live with the Seavers. Here again was a troubled teen, and DiCaprio devoured the role with his usual enthusiasm. "I liked the fact that he was homeless and didn't try to cover it up. He really was a nice, charming guy," Leo commented to a teen magazine of the time. "A street person isn't necessarily a bum or a depressed character. I felt that Luke gave people a more realistic image of someone in his position. He's witty and smart. Just like anyone else."

The program was performed before a live audience, and Leo loved that. He knew how to make silly lines funny, but more than that, he had the ability to pull genuine emotion from a character that could have been cardboard thin. He even learned to cry on demand for the role. For years, child actors in Hollywood had developed their own techniques to turn on the tear ducts—Shirley Temple simply thought of her pet dog dying, and the waterworks started. Leo found it a little embarrassing at first, but he only had to think of his mother horribly charred by a fire, and his eyes watered on cue.

By this time Leo had been granted a special home-schooling dispensation, which was probably a good thing because he was growing increasingly frustrated and difficult in class. The young actor finally had time to concentrate on the demanding schedule of the series. He describes his weeks on the show: "On Monday we would come in and do a cold reading. We just sat down and read our scripts around a

> He knew how to make silly lines funny, but more than that, he had the ability to pull genuine emotion from a character that could have been cardboard thin.

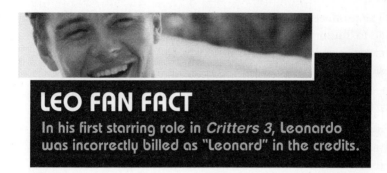

LEO FAN FACT
In his first starring role in *Critters 3*, Leonardo was incorrectly billed as "Leonard" in the credits.

table. Then we would go onto the set and start moving around with our scripts in hand. Then the next day we would go in and rehearse our 'sides' [individual script pages]. The third day we had all the words memorized. We would block everything—where we are going to move. Then we would practice all day before show time. We'd actually tape on Thursday without the audience in case there was a mess-up. It was pretty fun. More fun than filming every day. Then, on Friday, the curtain went up. We taped the show in front of a live audience, and you're really nervous."

The concern was that Kirk Cameron would take exception to this new kid who came in to take over his position as resident teen heartthrob. But Cameron, a Hollywood pro, had moved beyond that and warmly welcomed Leo to the set. The two got along well, and the ever-present teen magazines of the time reported that Cameron even helped DiCaprio to cope with his newfound popularity with the fickle teenage audience. In an interview, Cameron observed, "He's coping very well. We had long talks about it. One day we were walking outside the studio and some fans came up to us. We signed autographs and kept on walking. I told him to have fun with it. I was always grateful to the fans, and so is he. He's getting a lot of fan mail and trying his best to answer it all."

Leo's character was popular with audiences, but his presence was not enough to resuscitate the show. Its ratings continued to fall. After the seventh season, *Growing Pains* was dropped. A spinoff featuring Leo's character was discussed, but that went nowhere.

But the young actor's career was again leaping forward. He was actually excused from the last few episodes of *Growing Pains*.

The producers came up with the ingenious idea that Luke would go to Tucson to open a truck stop with his father. He just never came back. Leonardo DiCaprio was moving on to take his first starring role in the movies.

The film wasn't much. *Critters* was a low-budget 1986 horror film about a passel of fanged furballs who rolled along like deranged tumbleweeds, gobbling everything in sight while maniacally chuckling to themselves like the creatures from the movie *Gremlins*. Ironically, *Critters* starred Billy Zane, the man who, a decade later, would pursue Leo with gun in hand through the grand ballroom of the rapidly sinking *Titanic*. As is the way of these things, the moderately successful film spawned a series of cheesy sequels. In 1991, Leo was chosen to star in *Critters 3*. By then the writing, never much to begin with, had deteriorated considerably, and the monsters looked more like something a large cat had coughed up. Battling horrible dialogue, Leo could do little to save the film. It was so bad that DiCaprio has had it removed from his official bio.

The actor also refuses to talk about his next film. This one, *Poison Ivy*, starred Drew Barrymore and turned out to be a rather creepy tale of a sluttish teenager who is invited to move into a troubled household and seduces everyone in sight—with victims of both sexes. The impressive cast included Cheryl Ladd, Sara Gilbert and Tom Skerritt. Leo's role was so small that a couple of slices of the film editor's knife could have taken him out the film entirely.

It was probably DiCaprio's easygoing upbringing that made it possible for him to secure a coveted role in the first big-screen, big-budget film of his career, *This Boy's Life*. The first hurdle to overcome was the audition. It's hard to imagine any young actor not being overawed by reading for a part in front of Robert De Niro. The film was based on Tobias Wolff's 1989 memoir and details the abusive relationship between a stepfather and his new teenage son. Leonardo had already

> It was probably DiCaprio's easygoing upbringing that made it possible for him to secure a coveted role in the first big-screen, big-budget film of his career, **This Boy's Life**.

This Boy's Life (1993)

auditioned for the film's director, Michael Caton-Jones. The Scottish director had just released two successful American films: *Memphis Belle*, the story of the famous last run of the American B-17 bomber over Germany during World War II (again featuring Billy Zane) and the successful comedy *Doc Hollywood*, with former teen idol Michael J. Fox. But Caton-Jones was nervous about this serious film about human relationships firmly anchored in small-town America. Much of the film was to be shot in Concrete, Washington, where the author of both the book and the screenplay had lived the experience. Caton-Jones auditioned some 400 hopefuls, and Leo was just one of them. The young actor nailed the role on the second try. De Niro, the star and producer of the film, conducted the second audition. DiCaprio admits to being intimidated (he'd seen De Niro's *Raging Bull* five times), but he was determined not to show it. "I just stood up in front of De Niro, pointed at his face and shouted the lines at him. Then I sat there and waited for some kind of reaction. Everyone in the room started laughing, and I said 'What? What is it?' I guess the cool thing is I showed them I had something."

> **Later, the actor admitted, "I got the part by going in and doing it. No mumbo jumbo. I went in and looked him in the eye and got the part. I was confident, even though I had never done anything like that before. Now I realize it was ignorant confidence. I had no idea."**

The story has Toby, played by Leonardo DiCaprio, and his mother Caroline, played by Ellen Barkin, on the road. Leo tells us, voice-over on the soundtrack, that his mother has just left her latest abusive boyfriend, and they are on their way to a new life in Florida. When their car breaks down in Seattle, Caroline meets Dwight (De Niro) who seems to have an upstanding character and strong moral convictions. Caroline decides she has had enough running. Here is someone who promises security, a paycheck and a father figure for her sometimes-errant son. Closing her eyes to what

This Boy's Life (1993)

seems quite obvious to us, Caroline decides to settle down with this apparently caring man who soon demonstrates his real personality—that of an obsessive-compulsive. His target becomes his new stepson. It doesn't take long for this monster to turn physically abusive, and De Niro uses his considerable ability to threaten in order to heighten the tension.

DiCaprio's character, Toby, is struggling to discover who he is in the midst of this emotionally charged situation. "Toby was a little snot who needed someone strict," DiCaprio says. "But he didn't need a maniac like his stepfather Dwight. Dwight took strictness to a whole new level." The long-time movie pro and the new kid hit it off. Literally. DiCaprio told reporters that he had a few black and blue marks on his body before the shoot was over. In one scene, De Niro, a proponent of the method school of acting, gives his stepson a boxing workout and uses the occasion to teach the kid a lesson. Apparently, the two really mixed it up for the cameras. "I got a couple of bruises from big old Bobby D.," Leo observed with a grimace. "But he was very careful and nice about it."

Shortly before the release of the film, as broadcast entertainment journalist Jim Ferguson and I were walking down a hotel corridor during the press interviews for *This Boy's Life*, the door to a room opened. There stood a good-looking kid with a mop of unruly hair. He looked at us plaintively for a moment and then said, "Doesn't anyone want to talk to me?" With Ellen Barkin and Robert De Niro, to say nothing of the then hot Michael Caton-Jones, all vying for attention, the as yet unproven and unknown DiCaprio was being ignored. So the three of us sat and talked for the better part of an hour. *This Boy's Life* had turned the young actor around. He had originally been attracted to the business because of the huge sums of money that found their way into his stepbrother's pockets.

> "I don't know who I am yet or what kind of actor I want to be. I'm still in a stage of discovery."

But with *This Boy's Life*, he mused, he saw another side to himself. He was terrified for much of the shoot. "I really didn't know what I was doing. It was terrible. I'd go in there every day and learn how to be like that character and do the best I could." He spoke tentatively of his efforts to stay grounded. "It's kind of a weird feeling when people are defining you when you haven't even defined yourself. I don't know who I am yet or what kind of actor I want to be. I'm still in a stage of discovery."

The young actor was emotionally drained at the end of the long shoot but realized that more than anything, he wanted to act. Challenged by the demands of the role, he discovered that he could tap into a whole new set of raw emotions and feelings that he didn't know he was capable of. Said Leo, the 17-year-old who would grow up into something of a holy terror in his private life, "Don't let anyone convince you know who you are as a human being—because you don't. You're always changing and finding out new things about yourself. Don't get too comfortable in one way of being. That's one thing my father always told me."

He also said that during the production of the film, he was subject to one of the quirks that come with adolescence—a growth spurt. He shot up four inches, and in some scenes had to hunch down so he wouldn't look taller than the compact but rather short De Niro.

DiCaprio runs off with *This Boy's Life* even though he is co-starring with two of the most highly regarded actors of the time. And although the film did not set the box office on fire when it was released in 1993, Leonardo got the kind of reviews that kindle a career. "The movie is largely successful because DiCaprio is a good enough actor to hold his own in scenes with De Niro. The movie remains his story because he isn't upstaged by the loathsome but colorful Dwight," enthused Roger Ebert. Internet reviewer James Berardinelli observed, "DiCaprio…shows unexpected passion and raw ability."

The kid from the slums of Los Angeles was on his way. His next role was the toughest of his career, and this time, even the Academy Awards took notice.

chapter 4

I'm a miracle.
A walking miracle.

*—Arnie (Leonardo DiCaprio) to Becky (Juliette Lewis)
in What's Eating Gilbert Grape*

Walking into the room to interview Leonardo DiCaprio after viewing his next film *What's Eating Gilbert Grape* was an unsettling experience. Arnie, the character Leo plays in the film, was supposed to be 18 years old with the mental age of about four.

But the characterization the actor brought to the role was astonishing. For the movie, the intelligent, hip, aware and personable DiCaprio transformed himself into a boy with a vacant stare, a subtly altered face (with the help of a mouthpiece and shaggy haircut) and a carefree, jerky way of moving that let you know in every frame that he was a boy with little judgment and few inhibitions. Behind the actor's performance, you could see the innocence of a kid who would never grow up combined with the frustration of not being quite able to cope with a confusing world. The transformation was incredible.

Leonardo had learned the lessons of *This Boy's Life* well. It was obvious that this reluctant student was not going on to university—gone was the desire to study oceanography. But he was offered a major role in a surefire box office smash, *Hocus Pocus*, with the then red-hot Bette Midler. He didn't like the part or the script, but it was a chance to make a lot of money and move into mainstream moviemaking.

At the same time, Leonardo was fascinated by this small, quirky script that he received from a relatively unknown European filmmaker. Set in Endora, a small fictional Iowa town, its star was one of Leo's heroes, Johnny Depp, and there was, for him, the interesting role of a mentally challenged young man.

What's Eating Gilbert Grape (1993)

Leo opted for *What's Eating Gilbert Grape*, which proved to be one of the best decisions of his young life, since *Hocus Pocus* disappeared into a swamp of scathing reviews and box office disdain.

> At first, director Lasse Hallström didn't want DiCaprio. He felt the actor was too old and that his good looks would detract from the character.

Hallström was a subtle filmmaker with a back story of his own. He made the international art house favorite *My Life as a Dog* in his native Sweden. When I asked him why he would leave his home to make movies in America he replied sadly, "There is no Swedish film industry. If you want to make movies, you come to America." But Hallström's revenge was that he used the American movie machine's big dollars to make films with a distinctly European feel. The best example of this is *What's Eating Gilbert Grape*, which concentrates on character and moves with the slow, gentle pace of a film more often found in art houses.

Again Leo worked hard to secure the part. In a later interview, he said that he relied a lot on instinct. Hallström puts it this way: "It seems to come very easy to him. My theory is that he has a connection to the four-year-old inside him." Leo also spent considerable time studying the mentally challenged in an effort to understand Arnie. He watched videotapes and spent several days at a home for disabled teenagers. The actor was determined to show his character was not a stereotype. "I think people have these expectations that retarded children are really crazy," he said. "But it's refreshing to spend time with them. Everything to them is new and fresh. Arnie is spontaneous and carefree. He is also very needy. He has to be watched like a four-year-old, or he may do something that would hurt someone or himself. He really has no sense of right and wrong."

What's Eating Gilbert Grape is the story of the Grape family, who live in a small town in middle America. Johnny Depp plays

Gilbert, who is under great pressure despite living in seemingly quiet surroundings. First, there is his brother Arnie, who loves to sneak off and climb the local water tower. Not only are his actions highly dangerous, but they call out the local police who warn Gilbert that the next infraction may lead to Arnie being taken away to a home for the handicapped. Gilbert has two sisters who clamor and fight most of the time. Several years earlier, their father committed suicide and their mother (in a remarkable performance from actor Darlene Cates) ballooned up to about 500 pounds. As a result, she hasn't left her home in seven years. It becomes a game for local kids to sneak up to the windows of the Grape farm and try to catch a peek at the now mythical fat lady who lives there. In all the commotion, Gilbert tries to find some sort of emotional equilibrium in his off-kilter family, but he is having an affair with a local married woman (Mary Steenburgen) while holding down a dead-end job in a grocery store.

The high point of the brothers' year is when the annual Airstream trailer convoy comes through. In a powerful visual metaphor, the two stand by the side of the road and watch the sleek vehicles roar by, heading for…who knows where?

This particular year, one of the trailers remains in the local trailer park because of a mechanical breakdown, and Gilbert meets the vivacious Becky (Juliette Lewis). They fall in love, upending his carefully balanced life.

The film was intended to showcase Depp, and although the actor turns in his usual solid performance, it is DiCaprio that the audience remembers. His Arnie could have been lets-laugh-at-the-cripple funny or even a running sight gag, but instead, the actor gives a heart-wrenching performance of childlike wonderment as he wrestles with ideas and relationships beyond his ability to comprehend.

> The film was intended to showcase Depp, and although the actor turns in his usual solid performance, it is DiCaprio that the audience remembers.

LEO FAN FACT

One of Leo's favorite memories is of the time that he and his always-on-the-edge father joined "the mud people," a group of urban primitives who slathered themselves in mud, leaves and other organic material and staged "walkabouts" through the streets of Los Angeles.

Hallström's picture of rural America is heightened and colored by his outsider's view. His people aren't misfits because they don't see themselves that way. He gives you the feeling that they fit into Endora even though they would be dysfunctional outsiders in a big city.

Although set in Iowa, the film was actually shot in Texas. DiCaprio comments that the toughest thing was not making the movie but the long waits between takes. There was no nightlife or entertainment in the small Texas town, so the biggest enemy was boredom. "Juliette, Johnny and I talked about movies and acting and just hung out together a lot, but that was all we could do."

Although DiCaprio did not mention it during the interview, it's likely that two major consequences from that time continued to resonate in the actor's life. He learned from Depp, who refused to let his handsome face and quirky talent lead him into the career-killing quicksand of big-budget, mainstream starring roles. Depp told Leo to look for the interesting, challenging and creativity-expanding possibilities of smaller projects. (Depp, in fact, continued making art films like *Edward Scissorhands*, *Chocolat*, and *Benny & Joon* until he had sufficient clout in Hollywood to twist Captain Jack Sparrow in the big-budget *Pirates of the Caribbean: The Curse of the Black Pearl* into his own brilliant but off-the-wall shape). DiCaprio also watched Depp closely during his scenes, learning as much as he could from the seasoned actor.

The time in Texas was particularly hard on the gregarious, outgoing kid who grew up surrounded by friends and admirers in the middle of a big city. Cut off from friends and family, Leonardo was never so lonely in his life.

> **He decided that would never happen again, and from then on, in every contract he signed, there was a clause allowing him to fly some of his friends to the set no matter where it was. There in a tiny Texas town were sewn the seeds for "Leo's Posse," a gang that would terrorize bars, hotels and gin joints from Thailand to New York.**

When *What's Eating Gilbert Grape* was released in 1993, it surpassed all expectations at the box office. Everyone involved received great reviews, but again it was DiCaprio who came off best. *Movieline Magazine* observed, "DiCaprio does what Dustin Hoffman was trying to do in *Rain Man*." Said the *Washington Post*, "DiCaprio gives a tour-de-force, a marvelous, completely unselfconscious performance." Calling it one of the most enchanting movies of the year, Roger Ebert burbled, "DeCaprio's performance is both convincing and likeable. We can see why he's almost impossible to live with and why Gilbert and the rest of the Grapes choose to, with love."

> Said director Hallström, "I am convinced that he is, as you say in America, star material."

Even the venerable Academy of Motion Picture Arts and Sciences took note. In 1994, DiCaprio was nominated for a Best Supporting Actor Oscar. That year the competition was particularly tough. He joined such distinguished performers as Ralph Fiennes (nominated for *Schindler's List*), Tommy Lee Jones (*The Fugitive*), John Malkovich (*In the Line of Fire*) and Pete Postlethwaite (*In the Name of the Father*).

Despite his need for attention and company, Leo has always been afraid to stand in front of large crowds. The thought of appearing before millions on worldwide television terrified him. Still in his teens, the actor was afraid he would be unable to speak or that he would cry or say something to embarrass himself in front of the world. "I was dreading winning," he was to say later. "It was like this weight on my shoulders for so long. There were people saying, 'Hey, you might have a chance.' And I was going, 'No! No! I'm not gonna win.' I was trying to convince myself. I refused to plan a speech because I knew I was not going to win."

To bolster his courage, he took his mother, his stepmother and his father to the Oscars. Much to his relief, the award went to Tommy Lee Jones. "I wanted to get down on the ground and thank God," the happily jilted DiCaprio said later.

> Even the venerable Academy of Motion Picture Arts and Sciences took note. In 1994, DiCaprio was nominated for a Best Supporting Actor Oscar.

But the nomination had moved the young actor still higher in the Hollywood firmament. Not yet 20, he now had attracted not only an army of teenage girls awaiting the release of his next film, but he had also proven that he possessed the acting chops to take on just about any role he was offered. He was dating some of the loveliest women in the world—many of them considerably older than himself. Rumors circulated of affairs with supermodels and co-stars. The infamous posse was beginning to form around him, and few clubs worried about the age of their now-celebrated guest. For Hollywood's newest golden boy the future looked golden indeed.

chapter 5

...All right. Moment of truth. Somebody's life is going to change.

–Jack Dawson (Leonardo DiCaprio) holding the poker hand that wins him a ticket on the maiden voyage of *Titanic*.

Before he accepted the role of Arnie in *What's Eating Gilbert Grape*, Leonardo toyed with auditioning for the role of Malloy, the interviewer in *Interview with the Vampire*. Why not? The cast was intriguing—Tom Cruise, Brad Pitt and Antonio Banderas. The director was Neil Jordan, fresh off his triumph with *The Crying Game*. The screenplay was taken from the bestseller written by Anne Rice. But the role went to the older and more experienced River Phoenix.

He had always been fascinated by his father's stories of the free and easy hippie lifestyle of the '60s, and the film gave the actor a chance to enter a cinematic time machine and return to his father's fondly remembered youth.

Phoenix, a player in such films as *Indiana Jones and the Last Crusade* and *Stand By Me*, was falling victim to the easy seductions that Tinsel Town offers to the young, rich and famous. Unfortunately, a tragic event permanently removed him from the cast of that film.

Although the two never met, DiCaprio has a vivid memory of one near-encounter with Phoenix. "I was at a Halloween party. I remember it was really dark, and the place was packed. I was caught up in a lane of traffic, and I glanced over and saw this guy with a mask on, and suddenly I knew it was River Phoenix. I wanted to reach out and say hello because he was this great mystery, and we had never met. But then I thought he'd probably blow me off because I'd only done stuff by then that was just maybe worth watching. But then the lane of traffic started to move, and I slid right past him."

Later that evening, in the Viper Club, Johnny Depp's infamous Los Angeles swingers' watering hole, River Phoenix was in trouble. He made it outside to the fresh air, but that was as far as he got. He died of a drug overdose on the sidewalk in front of the club. He was 23.

> The role of Malloy suddenly came open. Apparently, the filmmakers hotly discussed Leonardo's name, but this was to be one of the few times Leo's ability to play and look young mitigated against him. He lost the role to Christian Slater. Leo remembers being disappointed, but a new project came along that seemed like it might be a lot of fun.

The Foot Shooting Party was an artsy short dealing with a young, early-'70s rock singer who shoots himself in the foot to avoid being drafted to the Vietnam War. The short (28-minute) film was to be produced by Renny Harlin, the Scandinavian director best known for action films such as *Cliffhanger* with Sylvester Stallone and *Die Hard 2* with Bruce Willis. The film also featured two other gifted young movie performers, Michael Rapaport and Jake Busey.

Leo's interest in the work was piqued by its portrait of the hippie central character. He had always been fascinated by his father's stories of the free and easy hippie lifestyle of the '60s, and the film gave the actor a chance to enter a cinematic time machine and return to his father's fondly remembered youth. Leo was costumed in the extreme fashions of the time and had extensions added to his locks to recreate the longhaired look. His appearance changed so much that it takes a moment to recognize the young actor onscreen. *The Foot Shooting Party* was designed as an experimental film, and apart from a few art-house showings, only a few people saw it. But Leo saw it as a tribute to his father and loved working on it.

The Quick and the Dead (1995)

By now the actor was becoming well known both for his teen-friendly, boyish good looks as well as his acting abilities. It seemed for a time that he was in line for every new blockbuster project that had a part for a young hunk. He turned down the role of Robin in *Batman Forever*, opting instead to look for more interesting material.

In 1995, actress Sharon Stone was riding high from her huge success with Michael Douglas in the sexy thriller *Basic Instinct*. With the box office clout she had built up, the actress could do almost anything she wanted, and what she wanted was a revisionist, feminist western called *The Quick and the Dead*. Her vision was to re-create the mythic qualities of the Clint Eastwood spaghetti westerns but with a tough-as-saddle-leather female as the lethal gunslinger. So she set out to assemble a dream cast and succeeded in surrounding herself with some of the best performers of the time. She enlisted Sam Raimi, who had gained a reputation as a director of stylish low-budget horror films like *Darkman* and *Army of Darkness* (Raimi eventually went on to achieve A-list status by directing the *Spider-Man* movies). As chief bad guy, she hired that master of lip-curling evil, Gene Hackman. She even summoned a then unknown Australian bloke named Russell Crowe to play a character who couldn't make up his mind if he wanted to be a gunslinger or a preacher.

To play the inevitable young kid, she wanted Leonardo DiCaprio. Leo was not impressed. "It was honestly not my idea of the type of movie I wanted to do next," he says. "I really had to think about it for a long time. I think I turned it down 20 or 30 times."

But Stone persisted. "All the other actors of Leo's age want to be cool and don't want to show any vulnerability onscreen," bemoaned the actress while pursuing the actor. And

> By now the actor was becoming well known both for his teen-friendly, boyish good looks as well as his acting abilities.

LEO FAN FACT

When Tri-Star Pictures waffled on Leonardo's salary demands, star Sharon Stone, who was also one of the producers, came up with the money herself.

DiCaprio, wanting to work with Stone's first-rate cast and crew, gave in and was soon strapping on his six-shooters. "I had this thing about not doing big commercial movies," he said harking back to his long conversations with Johnny Depp in Texas. "Most mainstream movies are crap—just pieces of garbage that have been done 1000 times over. But then I looked at *The Quick and the Dead,* and I thought, 'Okay.'" You can practically hear DiCaprio talking himself into it in an interview he gave at the time. "Sharon Stone is in it and—disregarding her stardom—the woman definitely has something going on. And Gene Hackman is in it, and Sam Raimi is a completely innovative director. My character is so completely insecure in himself that he has to put on a show to dazzle everybody."

In trying to re-create the mythic quality of the Sergio Leone westerns, the movie's plot tripped and fell on its own pretensions. Stone played Ellen, a female gunslinger out for revenge. She enters the annual quick-draw contest that John Herod (Hackman) runs every year in the small western town of Redemption. The kicker is that the quick draw is for real, and the winner is the last man (or woman) standing. Leonardo plays Herod's rebellious, unloved son who wants to impress Dad with his ability to slap leather. The actor practiced a lot with his six-shooter, and for a city boy from East L.A., became quite proficient at drawing and twirling his weapon. Eventually, he takes on a rough-looking customer and drills him on the spot. The young sharpshooter is then carried through the streets on the

The Quick and the Dead (1995)

townspeople's shoulders. The cocky kid is set for the showdown with the fastest draw of them all—the man he hates and loves the most at the same time—his own father.

The Quick and the Dead died at the box office faster than a loser in the quick-draw contest. It is a bizarre, rather unbelievable western but not hard to imagine Raimi toiling to give the work a production sheen. He turned the film into an exercise of angles, a how-to-do-it compendium of tricks and techniques, but it was all smoke and mirrors endeavoring to cover up an essentially empty story. Crowe played it straight and Hackman went over the top, but Stone was no Eastwood and proved as lifeless as her name. When the dust settled, DiCaprio again transcended the film to generate most of the good reviews. The *New Yorker* even called him a "young Jack Nicholson."

After the film, Gene Hackman had an interesting take on his co-star. "I didn't know DiCaprio's work. I was liking him very much on a human level—he was a cool and sensitive kid. On the other hand, he didn't know his lines. He seemed not to care about them, and I was not paying much attention to him. Up to the day where we shot this scene where he simulated his own death, the fantastic moment when he suddenly realizes he's gonna die. At this moment, I have been thinking, 'Wow! This kid can really act.' He's a marvelous actor. Success has nothing to do with it. He owns THE talent."

Although the rising young actor accepted his next film long before the dust settled on *The Quick and the Dead,* the decision comes off as a reaction to working on a big-budget Hollywood project.

> "Wow! This kid can really act. He's a marvelous actor. Success has nothing to do with it. He owns THE talent."

Jim Carroll grew up in the borderless world of New York in the 1960s. He was a rock musician and an accomplished writer and poet. He was also young, handsome and a member of a seemingly unbeatable high school basketball team. But he was seduced by easy access to drugs and spiraled downward into heroin addiction. Soon, he couldn't go home anymore and lived on the mean streets of New York, supporting his habit by robbing, stealing and prostituting himself. Carroll chronicled his own free fall and that of four of his friends in a series of journal entries, poems and essays that he later collected into a bestselling book called *The Basketball Diaries*.

The book moved from bestseller to cult status and stayed on the literary radar for years, a sort of latter-day *Catcher in the Rye* for a new, young and rootless generation. With its continuing sales and compelling story of youth and excess, it seemed a natural for the movies. A film company named Island Pictures finally acquired the rights. Although Leo had yet to win his Oscar nomination, his role in *This Boy's Life* impressed the company enough for them to offer him the lead role. "*The Basketball Diaries* was the first time I actually read a script that I didn't want to put down," said Leo.

The emerging star also liked the director. Scott Kalvert did not come up through the Hollywood ranks. He was a New Yorker who made his reputation producing videos—mostly for Marky Mark—who, under his real name of Mark Wahlberg starred with Leo in the film. When Leo's Oscar nomination came through, the deal was solidified.

So Leonardo DiCaprio went to New York for a new film. Along with the transcontinental journey came a change of lifestyle that was to earn him the title "Hollywood's Bad Boy."

chapter 6

Oh tumult! Oh Visions!
These are the steps of life.

–Arthur Rimbaud

It didn't take the New York tabloids long to discover that Leonardo DiCaprio was going to a drug counselor.

But as usual, in their search for screaming headlines, they got it all wrong. No, the kid just in from Hollywood wasn't hooked. He was only trying to get a handle on his role as a drug addict in *The Basketball Diaries*. He also spent hours on the basketball courts trying to learn the easy grace that marked Jim Carroll's basketball abilities, but no one was much interested in that either.

From his earliest days as a teen heartthrob, DiCaprio had been the target of rumors, innuendo and downright lies. Newspaper gossips, desperate for something to fill columns, had him paired up in steamy sexual relationships with most of his co-stars. The first was Juliette Lewis in *What's Eating Gilbert Grape*. When his character, The Kid, had a scene in which he woke up in bed with co-star Sharon Stone in *The Quick and the Dead*, the picture was published under such headlines as "Middle-Aged Movie Star Found in Arms of Teen Hunk." The same headlines later trumpeted a supposed liaison with Demi Moore.

But Leo was reaching an age when he was beginning to add fuel to the flame himself. His ever-present posse was always up to devilment. So far, mostly, it was just youthful high jinks, but gangs of teenage boys often find ways of horrifying their elders, and when your leader is the teen idol of the day, doors open that remain closed to other young men. The tabloids descended like sharks smelling blood.

"I love New York. I want to live here," was Leo's comment shortly after he arrived and

The Basketball Diaries (1995)

discovered the brusque attitude New Yorkers are famous for. "I came to New York and hung out while I getting ready for the role. It's very different from L.A. Out there, they tell you how great you are. Everyone flatters everyone. In New York, they put you down. They'll tell you the truth. It's good."

His co-star in *The Basketball Diaries*, Mark Wahlberg, had been one of the first white rappers, performing under the name of Marky Mark, and he knew the territory. He soon became a member of the posse, introducing Leo and his friends (who included Tobey Maguire, later to don spandex to become *Spider-Man*, and magician David Blaine) to the racy high life for which the Big Apple is famous. Jim Carroll, the subject of the film, actually enjoyed the way the actor portrayed him onscreen. "Oh, this guy's perfect," was his comment after seeing Leonardo's performance. But he has darker comments on Leo's co-star. "It was Marky Mark who introduced him to New York nightlife, and Leo just freaked out. He thinks you can stand on any corner in New York and have more fun than going to every club in L.A. I went to a club in New York, and I couldn't keep up with him."

The Basketball Diaries was a brutal, ugly film and demanded a great deal of focus and concentration from the actors. Although Leo worked hard at the role and gave it his best, his nights were an escape, spent tomcatting in the clubs, where he fast developed a reputation for being a party animal. One of the blessings that comes with being young is the ability to party all night and still function the next day.

Leo took to the New York scene with such alacrity, it seemed the actor didn't need to sleep. The tabloids and teen 'zines were quick to suggest that young Leo was following in the tragic footsteps of River Phoenix. Gossipmonger Liz Smith reported breathlessly, "Leonardo DiCaprio and

> "Out there, they tell you how great you are. Everyone flatters everyone. In New York, they put you down. They'll tell you the truth. It's good."

(co-star) Juliette Lewis—two lovebirds who seldom rest in the nest—were all over each other at The Rouge the other night." Even the magisterial *Rolling Stone* felt compelled to tut-tut. "He hits the Manhattan clubs and brawls with the locals. He seems poised to take over the mantle of River Phoenix."

Leo would eventually learn to ignore the press, but he was still young enough to be stung by the negative attention. He thought of himself as a normal fellow and was not sure how to cope with the constant stream of often untrue or highly exaggerated stories. "They want to title me as 'the young Hollywood hotshot, who all of a sudden goes rampant,'" he complained. "They don't see me hanging out in my hotel room or doing whatever normal things I do. I guess my mistake is thinking I can actually be like a normal human being and have fun and go to normal places. I'm realizing that I have to lead a sheltered life where I watch out for everything I do. I certainly don't think I'm leading a destructive lifestyle, at least compared with other people my age. I just try to loosen up a bit after work." (It should, perhaps, be pointed out here that Leonardo hated his hotel room and spent as little time in it as possible.)

> A hint of the bitterness that was later to taint his relationship with the press began to creep into quotes and conversations. In reference to his reported torrid affairs with co-stars such as Sara Gilbert and Juliette Lewis, he is reported to have said, "They're just my friends. Can't I have friends? But people want you to be a crazy, out-of-control teen brat. They want you to be miserable, just like them. They don't want heroes; what they want is to see you fall."

The Basketball Diaries (1995)

Leo never again spoke to the press with the openness he displayed in earlier interviews. Often on press junkets, as the other stars discussed their film, Leo hung around with his posse and ignored the entertainment journalists who were hungry for a quote. Sometimes the old Leo popped out, and he would greet a journalist like an old friend and return to the talkative friendliness of old, but that didn't happen often. He built walls in New York, and the once open, accessible kid from East L.A. disappeared behind them.

> **New York may have been where Leo's wild-boy reputation began to strike some sparks in the national consciousness but later, when he became the biggest star in the world, the sparks fanned into a conflagration.**

Meanwhile, he had a movie to make. Director Scott Kalvert may have grumbled a bit about Leo's high-octane nightlife, but everything he needed for his film was there in the rushes day after day. At only $4 million, *The Basketball Diaries* was a low-budget film by Hollywood standards. Gritty and real, Kalvert couldn't afford big sets, so he shot it documentary-style in filthy abandoned buildings and back alleys crawling with vermin. "It was chaos and pandemonium," Kalvert told reporters shortly before the film was released. "The kids were there in all the slime. They worked hard. They got grubby. They became real."

In one of the early scenes in the film, Leo (as Jim Carroll) and his teammates are sniffing cleaning fluid on the Staten Island Ferry—just a bunch of normal kids engaging in a highly dangerous practice for the fun of it. Carroll quickly sinks from after-school experimentation to a much lower level. His performance on the court deteriorates, and his home life becomes an endless battle with his mother (Lorraine Bracco), who finally, and in desperation, kicks him out of the house. His life becomes an endless round of crime, prostitution, uppers, downers, cocaine and heroin.

In the toughest role of his career, DiCaprio once again proves he and the camera were made for each other. With aching truth and believability, the actor takes us with him every inch of the way from vulnerable and promising athlete to gutter junkie. No matter where his mood swings lead—from ecstatic drug-induced high to suicidal lows—DiCaprio is entirely credible.

> "The movie took me places I'd never been before," he says of the experience. "Withdrawal was the hardest to play. It's like being an animal in a primal state."

Wahlburg is also impressive, moving with skill from music charts to movie screen. Bracco (who had received an Oscar nomination for Martin Scorsese's *Goodfellas*) is powerful as the devastated mother who has no idea how to cope with what is happening to her son. Others in the cast include Bruno Kirby, Ernie Hudson, Marilyn Sokol and Juliette Lewis (who plays a skuzzy hooker with sensitivity).

The image of Leonardo as someone who lives on the edge probably helped the film when it was released, but *The Basketball Diaries* was too raw for most audiences out for an evening of entertainment. It did not do well at the box office, nor did it find much acceptance among the critics who were divided on its merits. Some found it "wrenching" and "real," but other critics were less impressed by its unoriginal and oft-told story. Again, Leo received universally glowing reviews. Said Mike Clark in *USA Today*, "DiCaprio has so much presence that he almost saves the day." But neither his name above the title (for the first time) nor his incendiary performance could induce audiences to buy tickets.

After the release of *The Basketball Diaries*, the inevitable talk was of a movie about James Dean. Dean was a brilliant actor but

LEO FAN FACT

The Basketball Diaries was quoted as one of the inspirations for the Columbine school massacres. The two teen misfits Eric Harris and Dylan Klebold wore the same full-length trench coats that Leonardo wore in the film. Leonardo was horrified by the link, and it prompted him to tell his advisors not to accept any violent roles for him in the future.

a troubled young man who flashed briefly across the movie firmament in the mid '50s. He made only three films, *East of Eden*, *Rebel Without a Cause* and *Giant*, but it was enough to establish him as the "Next Major Star" and the personification of the restless American youth of the time. In 1955, the rebellious young actor ran his speeding Porsche Spyder headlong into another car and died on a California highway. Millions of young people who identified with Dean mourned his death, and he remains one of the iconic cult figures of the 20th century, continuing to reconnect with generations of young people who rediscover his movies. Ever since his spectacular flame went out, every handsome young man who emerges from the thousands who come to Hollywood each year looking for stardom is touted as the "next James Dean."

Warner Brothers was planning a big-budget film based on Dean's short but influential life, and Leonardo was the logical choice to play the role. Leo worshipped James Dean and, as a kid, often walked up the steep hill to the observatory in Griffith Park to the "hallowed" spot where the three ill-fated young actors Dean, Natalie Wood (who died in a rather mysterious drowning) and Sal Mineo (who died of knife wounds in 1976) shot their climactic scenes together in *Rebel*

Without a Cause. Near the observatory is a bust of Dean erected by his fans. Leo seriously thought about accepting the role for a time but finally turned it down. As far as he could see, the script called for a mere duplication of Dean's life, times and persona, and Leo wasn't interested in a role that allowed so little room for interpretation.

> **If young girls were waiting for Leo to make a film they could all flock to see, his next project would put a strain on them and his teen-'zine popularity. He was about to get his first screen kiss—from a man.**

Leonardo's role in his next film, *Total Eclipse*, was even more extreme and played against the sunny Southern California image the fan magazines had tried to promote for years. *Total Eclipse* depicted the short and unsavory life of the 19th-century French poet Arthur Rimbaud. Rimbaud, a gay wastrel and rebel, is highly regarded in France for his poetry and his doomed James Dean-like existence but is largely unknown in North America. The poet delighted in being rude and unmannerly and in making himself as obnoxious as possible in an effort to show his contempt for French society of the time.

But beneath his crude exterior beat the heart of a sensitive poet. Between the ages of 16 and 19, he wrote the beautiful, evocative verse that made him a hero to other disaffected young people who felt artistically stifled. He mailed eight of his poems to the respected poet Paul Verlaine, so impressing the older man that he immediately sent for Rimbaud.

> **Since Leo was beginning to push at the edge of his own society's conventions, he relished playing a revolutionary from another time. "To be that courageous!" exclaimed the actor.**

Instead of becoming the poetic mentor he imagined, Verlaine took one look at the youthful and sweet-looking

Rimbaud, left his young, rich wife and took up a self-destructive life of dissolution and depravity with his new love. As was the fashion for those who courted the high life of the time, the two began imbibing absinthe, a highly addictive drink distilled from the wormwood tree. Continued use was known to addle the brain, eventually leading to madness.

Ace British actor David Thewlis (Harry Potter's Professor Lupin in *The Prisoner of Azkaban*) played Verlaine, and Leonardo brought his youthful, open-faced vulnerability to the part of Rimbaud. The flamboyantly sexual relationship between the two men was graphically displayed onscreen. At one point, Leo's character leaps onto a table in a drinking establishment and displays his contempt for another poet's work by publicly urinating on it.

> **It wasn't the sort of thing guaranteed to bring big audiences into North American theaters, but what a challenge for the actor! Since Leo was beginning to push at the edge of his own society's conventions, he relished playing a revolutionary from another time. "To be that courageous!" exclaimed the actor. "Rimbaud wasn't blasé about anything. He did things that were unheard of. If I could just scratch the surface of that—I don't mean to compare myself with him, but I identify."**

Rimbaud ceased writing, flamed out and died a disgraced and ruined man at 37. Verlaine was also ruined, thrown into prison for "acts of perversity."

As for the graphic homosexual scenes, the exuberantly heterosexual DiCaprio seemed unperturbed. He offered enthusiastically before filming started, "I don't have a problem with doing a film about a relationship with another man. That's just acting, you know what I mean? But as far as the kissing stuff, that's really hard for me. I'm not kidding. But I've faced the fact that I've got to do it, and I'm gonna do it because, supposedly, I love the guy. But this movie is not about homosexuality, although I'm sure that's what the press is going to be all over."

Of course, he was right. During the filming, the tabloids, which were so seemingly outraged at his public displays of affection with supermodels and co-stars, decided that Leo just might be gay. Or at least bisexual. (Despite ample evidence of his sexual orientation, rumors of Leo's homosexuality had been circulating since *This Boy's Life*.) Predictably, in this case, pictures for the tabloid stories came mostly from the film. It is little wonder that Leo began to regard the press with great suspicion. To make matters worse, the public tends to confuse the character an actor plays with the actor—just ask any soap opera star.

Leonardo struck back defensively by talking to reporters he trusted, and soon the tabloids moved on to another star's supposed indiscretions. Said Leo, "It seems that artists aren't sure they are truly artists unless some big disaster happens. I pray that won't happen with me. I respect the gift, but acting is not the biggest deal in the world. If 'the gift' means disaster, I won't go there. There are no guarantees, but I won't end up like Rimbaud. You mark my words. So if you hear of any incident about me—a fight, a change of clothes, a little extra gel in my hair—don't believe it until you talk to me."

As for *Total Eclipse*? It was released in 1995, and in no time, it eclipsed as well. The total lack of audience appeal and critical disdain for the film did little to further Leonardo's career, but he still followed the Johnny Depp template

> "It seems that artists aren't sure they are truly artists unless some big disaster happens. I pray that won't happen with me. I respect the gift, but acting is not the biggest deal in the world."

and searched out roles that challenged and broadened him as an actor. He said after the movie's release and subsequent failure, "I like the film for what it is. If I had the opportunity to do it again, I would because it's such an interesting character to play. A lot of the time, real-life people are 100 times more interesting than anything writers can make up in their heads. And that character was one of the rebels. He revolutionized poetry by the time he was 16."

Perhaps Rimbaud's high lifestyle and sexual orientation affected Leonardo's choice for his next role. Or perhaps he saw it as one of the great challenges of his life and a chance to work with a hot new director. Whatever the influence, Leo was about to shift from homosexual free spirit to playing the most romantic lover in all of literature.

chapter 7

A pair of **star-cross'd lovers** take their life.

—Prologue to *Romeo and Juliet*

Leonardo DiCaprio was exhausted. He had been working steadily since he was a young teen, moving almost nonstop from project to project and set to set. Only 20 years old, he was already a millionaire. Perhaps it was time to go home and chill out for a while. Or, although he had survived three flops with his integrity and acting reputation intact, perhaps his career needed a positive jolt.

Leonardo always relied on his father for guidance in his choice of roles, and George was wildly enthusiastic about a radical MTV-style take on Shakespeare's *Romeo and Juliet*. Leo looked through the script, and although mildly interested, didn't bother looking at it again. George persisted, and Leo reread the script and suddenly caught the buzz. The actor was drawn by the sexy revisionist treatment Australian director Baz Luhrmann brought to the 400-year-old classic. In his international hit *Strictly Ballroom,* Luhrmann had proven he could take a well-used movie formula—the dance/love story—and put a new spin on it. Beyond that, he was an unknown quantity.

George and Leo flew to Australia to meet Luhrmann only to discover a creative tornado that spewed out an unending stream of ideas and visions. Leonardo signed up for a single workshop with the writer/director that stretched out to more than two weeks. By

> "I thought Leonardo was an extraordinary young actor, and I thought he'd make a great Romeo," Luhrmann said in an interview.

the time it was over, the two had cemented a lasting relationship, and Leo was committed to his first crack at the Bard. At first, his unfamiliarity with classical theater and lack of formal training worried him. From Lawrence Olivier to Mel Gibson, many accomplished actors have tried to bring Shakespeare to the screen, and joining that company was a daunting challenge. Also, Romeo is considerably more complex than he seems on the surface, and the worry is always that, like Hamlet, he is so well known that a weak performance might create an instant cliché.

But Luhrmann is something of a force of nature. "I thought Leonardo was an extraordinary young actor, and I thought he'd make a great Romeo," Luhrmann said in an interview. "He does seem to symbolize his generation." After spending considerable time working on the words together, Luhrmann convinced the young actor that he was quite capable of speaking Shakespeare's lofty poetry. "I wouldn't have done it if I had to jump around in tights," said Leo shortly before the movie was released. "You have this preplanned view of what the guy is supposed to be—just some fluffy, romantic kind of guy. But if you really study it, you see that Romeo was sort of like a gigolo who falls for this girl, Juliet. She says to him 'Look, if you've got the balls, put them on the table.' So he risks everything—his whole family, everything. And he marries this girl which is such an honorable thing to do if you believe in true love at that age. It's about all those things that carry you in a certain direction, and you can't stop; like when people run off to get married in Vegas. That's the beauty of it. They were both people who had guts. It's the ultimate love story."

Despite his energy, limitless imagination and persuasive ways, Luhrmann needed Leo as much as the actor needed the director. So far, William Shakespeare's *Romeo + Juliet* was just an idea in the charismatic director's mind. It may have been a modern, daring and innovative take on the famous tale, but it was not enough to persuade the producing studio, 20th Century Fox, to throw any money at the project. Luhrmann, acutely aware of how these things work, had videotaped the protracted workshop with Leo. The young actor's interpretation, in addition to his growing stature and popularity, persuaded the "suits" at Fox that Luhrmann could pull it all together, and they gave him a tentative green light.

This was no wimpy Romeo pining for his newly discovered love but a vibrant young man who was already a member of a violent street gang. Instead of placing the film in Shakespeare's medieval Verona, Luhrmann set his movie firmly in a mythical, decaying but vaguely Latino modern-day city (the location being Mexico City and environs). The license plates all read "Verona Beach." The characters speak the Elizabethan dialogue of the original but in the flat tones of contemporary American conversation. The opening shot has a television set with a commentator speaking the immortal lines of the Bard. The Capulets and the Montagues are feuding families who ride around in muscle cars with guns, rather than on horseback with swords and knives. The first time we see Romeo, he is standing on the beach bathed in the magic light of sunset that cinematographers love so much. By this time, Leo had lost much of the baby fat on his face that gave him such a youthful appearance; he looks every inch the romantic hero. We can easily believe that he is indeed Romeo, a man so passionate he is willing to die for love.

But such a dashing Romeo needed a Juliet who could sizzle alongside him. Luhrmann mounted a massive, worldwide search to find the right combination of fire, spunk and innocence. He auditioned some of the top young actresses of the day, including Alicia Silverstone (*Clueless*) and Natalie Portman (*Star Wars*' Amidala). Leonardo was equally committed to the process—he read with every actress who auditioned. It was Leo who steered Luhrmann toward Claire

Romeo + Juliet (1996)

Danes. He felt she had the right stuff to play a very young Juliet, who nevertheless had the determination to marry and ultimately kill herself for the man she loved.

Danes came to the audition with considerable experience and critical acclaim behind her. She had appeared in a failed pilot for a Dudley Moore television series but came to national attention as the disaffected teen in the series *My So Called Life*. The series had a short run on television, but reviewers consistently singled out her performance. She moved effortlessly into movies, appearing in *Little Women* and in other small film roles. She is probably best known as the sister in Jody Foster's richly comedic take on a supremely dysfunctional family, *Home for the Holidays*.

The chemistry between DiCaprio and Danes was obvious from the first audition. Of course, the usual rumors of an on-set romance circulated, but as Danes later told me at a special screening for the entertainment press held in Miami's trendy West Beach, their relationship never went beyond the bounds of friendly mutual respect. "We really clicked," she said. "It was great to find someone who really understands." Luhrmann expanded on that thought. He enthused in his broad Australian accent, "You can have two fantastic actors and still, the moment you see them onscreen, it's either there or it's not. They absolutely had it."

In Luhrmann's sleek, brilliant vision, DiCaprio's Romeo first spots Danes' Juliet through the glass of an aquarium during a masked ball held at the Capulet's home. She is dressed enchantingly as a gossamer fairy. Later, the famous balcony scene ("But soft, what light from yonder window breaks…") ends with the two of them plunging into a brilliantly turquoise swimming pool. Luhrmann's touch is everywhere. The lovers' first kiss is

> William Shakespeare's **Romeo + Juliet** is a sumptuous, color-drenched, eye-filling and ultimately heart-wrenching movie that brought credit, full houses and general (although not universal) critical acclaim to everyone involved.

in an elevator. Juliet's mother (Diane Venora) is an upwardly mobile, pill-popping alcoholic and Harold Perrineau Jr.'s Mercutio a drugged-out drag queen. The conflict between the Capulets and Montagues is depicted as more of a 1990s gang war than the familial power struggle of the original. And Pete Postlethwaite's Father Lawrence looks like an aging hippie priest the two lovers picked up somewhere on the beach.

The idea of pulling all these disparate elements, times and characters into a whole must have been a daunting one, but Luhrmann, with the help of his exemplary cast, made it work. William Shakespeare's *Romeo + Juliet* is a sumptuous, color-drenched, eye-filling and ultimately heart-wrenching movie that brought credit, full houses and general (although not universal) critical acclaim to everyone involved.

Romeo + Juliet (1996)

The making of the film was not without its problems. A sandstorm clocked at 90 miles per hour suddenly sprang up on the beach at Vera Cruz, stopping filming and blowing away several carefully built sets. An attack of killer bees and a case of food poisoning took four days out of Luhrmann's tight $15 million budget. And nearly everyone came down with dysentery.

Again, although Leo gave his all during the long days in front of the camera, he spent his nights living high with his ever-present posse. Wild parties were rumored to be videotaped by the participants for future viewing. One night the group, along with Danes, went out bar hopping. The evening escalated into a series of mishaps. The bouncer at a club picked a fight when he thought one of Leo's buddies was getting too boisterous, and the result was a couple of broken ribs—not the bouncer's. The same night, a crew member was hospitalized when a trio of men highjacked the taxi he was riding in, pushed the crew member's head into the pavement and threatened instant death if he didn't give them $400.

Leo was also something of a wild man on the set. He loved to imitate other cast members in their characters, which got laughs from the crew but unnerved some of the actors. An uncomfortable John Leguizamo (Tybalt) later complained, "I'd walk in front of the camera, and the first thing I'd hear were my own lines coming back at me in this high-pitched screech. I'd get really self-conscious when I had to deliver them for real." Leo moonwalked, did cartwheels behind the cameras and, remembers Claire Danes, "hit people over the head with Twizzlers."

> Leo was also something of a wild man on the set. He loved to imitate other cast members in their characters, which got laughs from the crew but unnerved some of the actors.

Fortunately, Leo's high spirits and practical jokes were confined to behind the camera. On camera, he was the perfect modern Romeo—handsome, ardent and committed. A dedicated smoker himself, Leonardo played Romeo as a chain-smoking, poetry-spouting rebel who finds himself hopelessly caught up in the throes of love. "I think," he opined, "Shakespeare would have wanted his work to live on through the years and become a timeless piece that could adapt to the future."

Apparently, audiences agreed with him. When it was released, *Variety* had the film at number one at the box office with a first weekend take of $36 million. By the time its (North American) theatrical run ended, the movie had amassed something upwards of $50 million—not a bad return on an investment of $15 million. Leonardo celebrated his 22nd birthday the same weekend as the initial release.

> "Luhrmann and his two bright angels have shaken up a 400-year-old play without losing its touching, poetic innocence," enthused Peter Travers in **Rolling Stone**.

New York playwright Scott McPherson had actively nursed several of his friends who were dying of AIDS. As therapy for himself, he turned his experiences into a play, *Marvin's Room*. Although not specifically about AIDS, it was about death and dying, and McPherson drew heavily on his own experiences. The play provided strong roles for actors of both sexes and, in 1992, ran for a respectable 214 performances on Broadway. That same year, shortly before McPherson himself succumbed to AIDS-related complications, he turned his metaphorical work into a screenplay.

It was obvious that *Marvin's Room* was never going to rule at the box office but, like many Woody Allen movies, it provided a challenge for actors, and some of Hollywood's best began to circle the property. Once again Robert De Niro was set to produce. Almost immediately Diane Keaton, Hume Cronyn, Meryl Streep, Gwen Verdon and Leonardo signed on. Once again, Leo would play a troubled teen—Hank, Streep's wayward son, who douses the family album in lighter fluid and sets it (and the house) on fire. When we first see him, he is in a mental hospital in restraints.

Streep and Keaton play estranged sisters. Twenty years earlier, Lee (Streep) flees after envisioning a bleak future as a caregiver to Marvin, her terminally ill father (Cronyn). Bessie (Keaton), unmarried and alone, stays behind to care for Marvin and her somewhat dotty aunt (Verdon). The two sisters hadn't spoken since Lee left. But Bessie's rather befuddled doctor (De Niro, in an uncharacteristically semi-comedic role) tells her she has leukemia and that her only hope may be a bone marrow transplant from a family member. This leads to the inevitable and uncomfortable reunion of the two sisters.

The film is that rarest of movies, the intelligent tearjerker, giving an intimate portrait of a supremely dysfunctional family in crisis. Streep, consigned by great cheekbones and overwhelming talent to playing characters with a great deal of class, reveled in portraying "trailer trash." For his part, DiCaprio enjoyed the challenge of playing with a company of the best actors in the business.

"Meryl Streep is completely unlike any other actress I've ever worked with," he said later as he was hanging with his posse in the hallway of the hotel in Austin, Texas, where the press junket was held. "Just because I've never met anyone who could walk onto a set—without saying anything—and have complete and utter respect. I mean, everyone becomes silent when she walks in, and it's this thing when she acts. When I did my first scene with her, she was sort of all over the place doing things. I was like, 'What IS she doing?' It seemed so unlike anything I've seen before. How is that going to look on camera? But even if she seems to be doing some wild things sometimes, everything looks real and natural on camera. It was a big shock to me because I've never worked with an actress like that."

The always accommodating and friendly Streep was equally impressed with DiCaprio's work. "He's always compelling to watch," she said. "You can't watching anything else when he's acting."

Marvin's Room was Broadway director Jerry Zaks' first film. He opened up the original play, and the result was a film that could have been saccharine and melodramatic but instead was kept real by strength of performance and controlled, intelligent direction.

LEO FAN FACT
Marvin's Room was the first and only movie ever to be shot in Florida's Walt Disney World.

Marvin's Room surpassed all box office expectations. Everyone involved garnered superlative reviews, and Keaton was nominated for an Academy Award.

On a chilling personal note, in June of that year, Leo had something of a life-altering experience. Seeking an adventure, he decided to jump out of a plane. So, he dove into a cloudless cobalt-blue sky 1200 feet above the California desert. As instructed, he pulled the ripcord on his parachute. Nothing happened. A terrified Leo fell helplessly to the ground below. Luckily, he was falling in tandem with his instructor Harley Powell, who motioned to Leo to pull the release on his backup chute. It blossomed like some exotic life-giving flower, and Leo glided to a gentle landing. He was later quoted as saying, "I like doing things that scare me, but skydiving is just the sickest thing. I made a little video afterward where I go all jittery in the camera, and I go, 'Leonardo, if you're watching this, this is your last time skydiving. It's your first life-and-death experience. I want you to learn something from this.'"

Just one year later, an adventure of a different kind awaited him on the world's most opulent ship on a course with death in the frigid North Atlantic.

chapter 8

I figure **life is a gift**, and I intend to take advantage of it.

—Jack Dawson (Leonardo DiCaprio) to a table of the very rich in the Grand Salon of *Titanic*.

Leonardo DiCaprio was going through his usual self-induced torment. Should he take the role of Jack Dawson in James Cameron's huge studio production (actually it took two studios—Paramount and 20th Century Fox—to come up with the money) about the maiden voyage and subsequent sinking of the *Titanic* or continue to look for a smaller role playing another conflicted young man? *Titanic* stood for everything Leo disliked about Hollywood—the sort of bloated, big-budget feature he often put down during interviews.

But Jim Cameron was an interesting filmmaker. The story was intriguing. He thought that it might be challenging to play it straight as a romantic hero. And then there was that $1 million paycheck.

Kate Winslet takes the credit for pushing Leo into the role. The beautiful young woman with the impeccable classical credentials (Ophelia in Kenneth Branagh's four-hour *Hamlet* and an Oscar nomination for *Sense and Sensibility*) was the first major star cast. "I knew Leo was thinking about it," she told interviewer Charlie Rose. "I remember tracking him down at [the] Cannes [Film Festival] and told him we'd have fun. And thankfully he said yes to it."

The two knew each other slightly, but the first scene shot was an experience for both performers. "I was naked in front of Leo the first day of shooting," Winslet confides in the bestselling book, *James Cameron's Titanic*. "It almost always happens that some of the most important scenes get shot at the very beginning when you are just getting to know each other." "Kate is great," enthused Leonardo. "She had no shame with it. She wanted to break the ice a little bit beforehand, and so she flashed me. I wasn't prepared for that so she had one up on me. It was pretty comfortable after that."

"How am I doing so far?"
joshed Leo when shooting ended.

Shot back the director, "Well, you know. It's only your first day. We can always recast."

Titanic had long been an obsession with Canadian-born writer/director/producer/technical visionary Jim Cameron. He'd made his reputation turning out seamless, expensive-looking sci-fi films with small budgets. After creating a career for Arnold Schwarzenegger in the first *Terminator,* he brought his creepy follow-up to *Aliens* in for only $18 million. By 1991, his reputation was such that he could lavish $93 million on *Terminator 2* and more than $100 million on *True Lies.*

Nothing could stop Cameron in his quest to film the fateful voyage of the RMS *Titanic.* He spent two years of his life and $4.5 million assembling, and in some cases, inventing equipment that would allow him to photograph both inside and outside the broken body of the *Titanic* itself, the rust-covered hulk on the seabed two and a half miles below where she'd hit that iceberg. Cameron descended time and again to the eerie wreck, free falling for two and a half hours through inky blackness in a tiny three-man submarine. He used the footage he shot as an IMAX 3-D big-screen feature, *Ghosts of the Abyss,* and to bookend his film about the first and last voyage of the "ship of dreams." The writer/director was intensely moved by the sight of the actual decks where the passengers perished. "I realized," he said, "that my project, my film was doomed to failure if it could not convey the emotion of that night rather than just the fact of it. My most daunting task was not the creation of a great spectacle. It was the fashioning of the intimate moments both during the writing and subsequently working with Kate and Leonardo. The three of us knew, to our ongoing terror, that the fate of our *Titanic* lay in our ability to steer her properly past the icebergs of bombast and to create a living heart for the film out of gestures, glances, tentative smiles, halting awkward sentences…the vocabulary of nascent love."

> But let us concentrate for a moment on the spectacle. With his record of making big-budget films that spun fortunes at the box office, Cameron was able to squeeze out a budget of more than $100 million, one of the biggest ever for a movie up to that time (although Cameron likely went into his production using the budget as a guideline rather than a final figure).

It was still something of a risk. Would anyone pay to see a movie where the outcome is already known and almost everyone dies? Several films about the tragedy were already out there playing the late show, and a Broadway show based on the same topic was running. Cameron was shooting for a film length of over three hours. Would mainstream audiences, used to the flash and dash of current effect-heavy movies, sit still that long?

But the story of the *Titanic* was too fascinating to leave at the bottom of the sea. Built between 1910 and 1912 at a then unheard-of cost of $7.3 million, *Titanic* was the most opulent ship of her time. On April 14, 1912, five days into its maiden voyage from the British port of Southampton on her way to New York, she struck an iceberg and sank. Nearly 1600 people died. Only 700 survived.

In his foreword to the bestseller written about the making of the film Cameron observes, "*Titanic* still captures our imaginations after 85 years because her story is like a great novel that really happened. The story could not have been written better…the juxtaposition of rich and poor, the gender roles played out unto

Titanic (1997)

death (women first), the stoicism and nobility of a bygone age, the magnificence of the great ship matched in scale only by the folly of the men who drove her hell-bent through the darkness. And above all, the lesson: that life is uncertain, the future unknowable...the unthinkable possible."

Although the final film is special-effects heavy, Cameron did not want his actors to pantomime in front of a green screen. He had a almost life-size version of *Titanic* built in a special studio he constructed on the ocean in Rosarito Beach, Mexico. The studio also contained soundstages and sophisticated production facilities. (Called the Fox Baja Studios, it continues to be used for such water-soaked epics as *Master and Commander*). At 780 feet long, the *Titanic* model was an awesome 90 percent to the scale of the original. The ship had to sink and rise again many times, so it was mounted on massive pneumatic jacks in a 17-million-gallon oceanfront tank. The original 1911 designs of *Titanic*'s builders Harland and Wolff, thought to be lost, were located and used to build the model. Intricate smaller versions of both the original and the wreck on the ocean floor were built on soundstages in Hollywood and Mexico. Huge, ornate sets were constructed—sets that were eventually to be destroyed by the inrush of seawater. At one point, 90,000 gallons of water from overhead dump tanks were poured into the re-created grand ballroom. The water crashed through the domed skylight with such force that it tore the grand staircase from its steel foundations, luckily on camera.

And at the center of all this lay the simple love story of the scruffy artist and adventurer Jack Dawson and the genteel, upper-class Rose DeWitt Bukater. Just before the great ship sails, Jack wins a ticket for the maiden voyage in a card game. It doesn't take him long to become bored with his Spartan steerage-class surroundings, and he goes to

> The ship had to sink and rise again many times, so it was mounted on massive pneumatic jacks in a 17-million-gallon oceanfront tank.

explore the ship. At the stern, he sees Rose. Rose's mother (Frances Fisher) is desperately trying to pull the family out of debt by marrying off her daughter to an arrogant but extremely rich cad, Cal Hockley (Billy Zane). Rose has grown to despise Hockley, and seeing an empty life before her, tries to throw herself into the ocean. Jack rescues her, and the two are immediately attracted to one another.

The haughty Cal, thinking he might have some sport with the lower-class Jack, invites him to supper with some of his rich friends, but Jack, besides looking gorgeous in his borrowed formal attire, is also charming and funny.

Rose loses her heart and the pair has a steamy liaison in a vintage car in the hold of the ship. Soon afterwards, however, the *Titanic* lightly scrapes an iceberg, but it is enough to puncture her metal skin, and the great liner begins her slow, inexorable two-hour-and-forty-minute slide into the frigid Atlantic. Jack is falsely accused of theft and is shackled to pipes in an office deep inside the ship. As she sinks and the office fills with water, Rose must devise a way to free Jack so they can fight their way to the deck. Of course, when they get there, it's too late. *Titanic* is upended; hundreds have already perished; and the lifeboats are gone.

The length and difficulty of the shoot drove Leo and Kate together. They became best friends—although both are quick to point out—nothing more. "I love Leo to bits," says Kate. "The first time our lips touched, we were both like 'ooooh …yuck.' I told him, 'I feel like I'm kissing my brother.'" In a later interview, she did allow, "Leo is stunning. He is even more gorgeous in the flesh than he is onscreen."

"It was the toughest shoot," recalls Leonardo. "It lasted six or seven months, and Kate and I were driven very hard in a lot of difficult water scenes." With cast and crew up to their necks in freezing water, Leo felt there wasn't much use in complaining. Everyone was…well…in the same boat. "It was costing a fortune," the actor goes on, "so we did all our complaining in private, with just of the two of us. We did not have to vent it on anyone else. Sometimes Kate was in tears, sometimes I was and occasionally we both were. It was that kind of job. Kate is awesome, beautiful and talented and really down to earth."

Some moments were genuinely dangerous. At one point, Kate and Leo were running down a long hallway in front of a huge wall of water. They came to a locked gate which they managed to get open, but Kate's long dress caught on the bottom of the gate and pulled her underwater. "I had to shimmy out of my coat to get free," remembers Kate with a shiver. "I had no breath left. I thought I'd burst." One night Kate and Leo were secured to a railing for a shot when a big storm blew up. The crew fled, forgetting that the two stars were tied and couldn't move. It was a long hour before they were freed.

Rumor had it that Cameron drove his crew unmercifully, with reports of broken ribs and sprained ankles. *Time* magazine reported on the large numbers of injuries, and the Screen Actor's Guild sent a special representative to assess the situation. They found nothing improper in the safety standards, but the visit did invoke an impassioned letter from Cameron to the *Los Angeles Times* in which the director argued, "With every film I make, I try to challenge myself as an artist and technician, to push myself beyond what I have done before. I enlist a team of people around me who likewise welcome the opportunity to test themselves, their skill, their craft and their personal endurance." Said one member of the production team, "Jim will put himself in danger before anyone else."

> He felt they needed to feel the decks under them and experience the size of the ship around them in order to wring from them the expansive and real performances he wanted.

But, like on any set, it's the sitting around and waiting that crushes the spirit more than anything else. Leo entertained cast and crew with his impressions or just generally clowned around. "Working with Leo

LEO FAN FACT
Winslet's gift to DiCaprio after the film was a warm fleece blanket.

was like having a little brother on set," the affable Billy Zane recalls. "It got pretty silly. We were into hallway bowling."

> "The best is, truthfully," Leo admits, "the few minutes when you're on set, and you feel like that character. You're really there, and it seems like reality. For me, it only happens once or twice on a whole film, where I go, 'Wow! I am this guy.' You get in a zone, and just for those moments, it's incredible."

One of the reasons Cameron kept special effects to a minimum and staged most of his movie on giant sets was to give the actors the feel of the scope of the event. He felt they needed to feel the decks under them and experience the size of the ship around them in order to wring from them the expansive and real performances he wanted. "When I first saw it," offers Leonardo, "there's a whole world that goes on while you're doing your stuff, and I didn't want to focus on that. Otherwise I would have been overwhelmed. I needed to do just what I needed to do and to make this character as real as possible and concentrate on our little story that was going on. There were times of madness," he goes on, "sitting strapped onto the back of the hydraulic poop deck with Kate, surrounded by 20 cranes and the director swooping in at us. As we were doing our lines and screaming, part of me was thinking, 'Am I crazy?'"

The huge set was ringed with hot tubs so that the frozen actors could leap in to get warm after their scenes in the frigid ocean waters. One particularly surreal scene had hundreds of frozen corpses rise from their watery graves between set-ups and climb into the hot tubs in full costume and make-up looking like zombies with icy hair, frozen blue faces and fingernails.

Titanic was scheduled for release on July 4, 1997. But because Cameron demanded perfection in postproduction and special effects, the opening was put off until November. This kind of delay is generally perceived in Hollywood as a bad sign—a film in trouble and undergoing last minute tinkering. Meanwhile, Cameron's budget blossomed past the $200 million mark, making *Titanic* the most expensive film ever produced.

The mega-movie finally premiered in Japan on November 1, 1977. Thousands of Japanese girls lined the roads leading to the theater screaming "Leo, Leo, Leo." Reports filtered back to North America of an epic adventure with a beating heart, but when the film opened in the U.S. the week before Christmas, initial reviews were mixed, and its $28.6 million at the box office was something of a disappointment, considering that the comedy *Scream 2* had spun the turnstiles to the tune of $33 million the week before.

But the miracle slowly began to unfold. Instead of going down, revenues from the film went up and up and up. The buzz began. Week after week, the film maintained its place at number one at the box office. It held there strongly for 15 weeks. *Titanic* remained in the Top 10 for a record-breaking 26 weeks, making over $1 billion at the box office and sailing past all the excess and exaggeration to become the most successful film of all time.

> Leonardo was being hailed as the Clark Gable of his generation. The onscreen relationship of the two stars was celebrated as the greatest since Gable and Vivian Leigh in **Gone with the Wind**.

Leonardo was being hailed as the Clark Gable of his generation. The onscreen relationship of the two stars was celebrated as the greatest since Gable and Vivian Leigh in *Gone with the Wind*. "Genuinely affecting," burbled *People* magazine. Enthused *Entertainment Weekly*, "When people talk about movie magic, this is what they mean." At Oscar time, *Titanic* was nominated for 14 Academy Awards including Best Film. Kate Winslet was nominated for Best Actress. Notably missing was Leonardo DiCaprio. "Oscar Sinks Hunk…Heartthrob, Leonardo DiCaprio is Snubbed" proclaimed the *New York Daily News*.

Leonardo DiCaprio chose not to appear at the Los Angeles Shrine Auditorium on March 23, 1998, to watch Jack Nicholson walk away with an Oscar for his performance as the obsessive-compulsive Melvin Udall in *As Good As It Gets*. He didn't see *Titanic* win its 12 Academy Awards. Or see it chosen as Best Film or hear James Cameron's now infamous "I am the king of the world!" speech when he accepted the statuette for Best Director. Leonardo left town. He was chided in the press for being a poor sport, and Cameron made a comment about Leo "not being a team player."

Gabriel Byrne (on Leonardo being overlooked for an Oscar nod for *Titanic*.): "Leo doesn't need an award to validate his talent; his acting speaks for itself."

But Oscar or not, life would never be the same for Leonardo DiCaprio.

chapter 9

I'll never let go, Jack...
I'll never let go.

—Rose to Jack in the frigid waters of the North Atlantic after the sinking of the *Titanic*.

Leonardo DiCaprio was leaving the Charles de Gaulle Airport in Paris when a young girl attached herself to his right leg. She was one of hundreds who had appeared when they heard the star of *Titanic* was passing through. She managed to burst through security, and for a moment, was ONE with her idol.

When he couldn't disengage her, Leonardo tried reason. He bent down and earnestly explained that he was only Leo, the kid from East Hollywood, not Jack Dawson the doomed artist of the movie. It was all to no avail, and the authorities had to peel her from Leonardo's leg.

By now Leonardo and Kate Winslet were probably the most recognizable faces in the world. Even in eastern countries, ruled by iron-fisted Islamic governments that banned movies, copies of *Titanic* were being passed hand to hand. When the Taliban were driven out of Afghanistan, posters of Leonardo began appearing on living room and, presumably, bedroom walls. Winslet tells of walking in the foothills of the Himalayas when a nearly blind and very old man came up to her and asked "You *Titanic*?" But Winslet never reached the Everest-like heights of celebrity that were visited upon her co-star.

To uncounted millions all over the world, Leonardo was the hero of their dreams. To young

> Until you see it in real life, the raw power of the celebrity phenomenon is unfathomable. It is a monster that can never be satisfied, and those who are held in its powerful grip cannot escape.

boys, he was the combination of mythic adventurer (and chick magnet) that they wanted to be and the party-hardy Hollywood movie star who did what he wanted while cavorting with beautiful models and actresses. To many girls, he was the most impossibly handsome man-boy in the world—young enough to be accessible, yet worldly and independent. Many a young girl's bedroom was converted into a shrine for Leo, complete with photos and votive candles. Insatiable fans saw the film over and over again, much the same way that Christian pilgrims used to travel to Lourdes or Muslims to Mecca. One young fan quoted in *Teen People* said, "I was moved to tears that never seemed to stop. I never cried more in a theater in my life. It wasn't just a movie, it was a life experience."

The roots, causes and results of celebrity, from Rudolph Valentino through Frank Sinatra and James Dean to the Beatles, have been probed elsewhere. Hundreds of screaming young girls line up at premieres or plaster themselves against wire fences at airports just hoping for a glimpse their hero.

Until you see it in real life, the raw power of the celebrity phenomenon is unfathomable. It is a monster that can never be satisfied, and those who are held in its powerful grip cannot escape. Suddenly, Leonardo couldn't go anywhere. The popular press affixed themselves to his growing celebrity like leeches to a swimmer in a lake. Phalanxes of cameramen camped out near his home. When they couldn't get a picture of Leonardo, they hired look-alikes to stand in front of his house or a downtown club, and they sold the pictures as real. They rented helicopters and turned every car trip Leo took into a caravan of madmen weaving in and out of traffic and waving cameras.

In New York, the paparazzi use a trick to get the "money shot" for their tabloid employers. At movie premieres, where they know their target is supposed to attend, they join the batteries of

The Man in the Iron Mask (1998)

photographers lining the red carpet, and then as Leonardo (or Julia Roberts or Brad Pitt) walks by, they scream vile, foul-mouthed epithets at them, hoping the stars will recoil with horror as the paparazzi snap a shot. The background in the picture is then digitally altered at the lab to make it look as if the star was found in a compromising situation. The final result is emblazoned on the front page under a headline that might read, "Hollywood Hunk Found in Love Nest with Underage Fan." The story, of course, is a complete fabrication.

In keeping with a long-time Hollywood tabloid tradition, one good story is worth a thousand true ones. But the stars soon learned to float through the pandemonium around them like European royalty with their press people picking the "right" media and pre-set groups of fans to stop and talk to.

The latest are the squads of enterprising techno-geeks who have learned to hide the new state-of-the-art, fiber-optic lipstick cameras on their persons and then try to pass themselves off to the keeper of the velvet rope at various clubs as "friends of Leonardo." In this day of the digital phone, the hangers-on, wannabes, groupies and paparazzi know almost immediately when Leonardo is on a night out with his friends. The baby paparazzi try to sit near the star in hopes of catching him on tape doing drugs, getting drunk or making out with some starlet. Unproven wild rumors have circulated of Leo engaging in overt sexual activities in the clubs with everyone from Claire Danes to

Carmen Electra—then in an on-again-off-again marriage to flamboyant basketball star Dennis Rodman. Leonardo told one entertainment journalist, "They had us kissing and making out all night when I think we said hello. Someone at the bar sold the story."

Of late, most of the trendy watering holes where Leonardo and other hip young Hollywood players, rock stars, models, sports heroes and others just along for the ride hang out have private rooms for their "special guests." No photographers are allowed in, making for a kind of uninhibited freedom for those whose presence often causes a furor. But even in private rooms there is little escape from those who would manipulate the publicity machine. A favorite trick for the manager of an up-and-coming starlet or model is to have them strike up a conversation with the girl-friendly Leonardo, knowing that even if it only lasts a few moments, her picture (probably in a skimpy bathing suit on a beach somewhere) will be a prominent feature in the tabloids the next day with a caption that might read, "Rising Hollywood starlet may be Leonardo DiCaprio's new love."

While making *The Beach* in Thailand, the media breathlessly reported that Leonardo had impregnated his comely co-star, France's Virginie Ledoyen. Then when a jellyfish stung him, they embellished the simple truth into a bloody tale of how the star had been bitten by a shark.

One enterprising English journal had Leonardo being offered $33 million to star in a sequel to *Titanic*, blithely ignoring the fact that the ship had sunk and that Leo's character had died in the first film.

Leonardo had nowhere to hide. He became prisoner to his own myth. When in Rome shooting *Gangs of New York*, he had to stay holed up in his hotel room

> We will never know how the fun-loving young man who just wanted to be a good actor in small movies was coping. His anguish and pain were private and lived out in the houses and hotels where he was trapped.

because hundreds of screaming young people gathered outside in the street. His co-star Cameron Diaz marveled at the spectacle as it spiraled ever more out of control. "It makes his world really small, and I totally feel for him," she said sympathetically. "To have so much and then because of that to have so little at the same time. I don't understand why people hang outside his hotel all night. But when people become fanatical like that, you can't help but feel that you're responsible for them in some way. I think that it's very odd and very selfish of those people to keep someone prisoner like that. You know, for a lot of these girls that are out there in front of his hotel, nothing Leonardo does is enough for them. He can't come outside and say hello enough times; he can't do anything enough times. I think it's unfair that he is kept almost like a prisoner because of them."

Leonardo took Claire Danes with him to the world premiere of his film *The Man in the Iron Mask*. "I'm just at the edges of Leomania," observed the actress, "and I'm feeling the energy and the heat and the intensity of what's happening to him. It's petrifying. [At the premiere] he got up and walked across the room to see his mother, and the entire side of the room stood up and followed him. There were 60 people, and they just followed him. It was beyond weird."

> It's such a shame," commented Leo's close friend Mark Wahlberg. "He's such a nice guy. I hope he will be able to cope with this madness."

We will never know how the fun-loving young man who just wanted to be a good actor in small movies was coping. His anguish and pain were private and lived out in the houses and hotels where he was trapped. In the long run, he obviously was coping because he came through it mostly intact. But it was tough. Especially in the beginning, when he felt he was the same person he had always been, even if the world saw him as some silver-screen icon to be venerated. In the few interviews he gave, he continually expressed his desire to be known as a street-bred, hardworking character actor. As time went on and the press reports grew more and more outrageous, and Leomania

The Man in the Iron Mask (1998)

expanded to even more dizzying heights, he withdrew. "Everything I've done since *Titanic* has mutated in the press," he said, reflecting sadly on those hectic years. "At first, I was shocked to see how eagerly people are willing to lie just to sell a story. Now I just accept it. You can't take anything that is written about you personally. You can't freak out, or it will eat you alive. Rumors are so hurtful and insidious that you just have to smile and ignore them. At first, I tried to get my press people to counter the rumors with the truth, but that only fuels the fire. I'm going to let my work speak for itself. The work is the reason I became an actor in the first place. I've always had this insane desire to perform for people. *Titanic* has put me in an incredible position, and I'm not going to let this celebrity thing destroy it for me."

Immediately after *Titanic*, Leonardo went into a handsome remake of *The Man in the Iron Mask*, mostly because he wanted to work with a quartet of movie stalwarts—Jeremy Irons, Gabriel Byrne, Gérard Depardieu and John Malkovich. "It was so cool working with people of that caliber because they are so relaxed about everything. They're almost like children in a sense; it's fun for them at this point. And it was totally cool working like that," Leonardo told an interviewer. The actor played two roles in the costume drama based on Alexandre Dumas' classic adventure novel about France's King Louis XIV and his evil twin brother. Leonardo relished the idea of playing a classical villain for the first time. Randall Wallace, who had written Mel Gibson's *Braveheart*, directed the film.

There were indications of what was to come while Leonardo was shooting in France. Long an art lover, he decided to visit the Louvre in Paris. But he had to leave that venerable art institution because he was spotted by packs of young girls who then chased him through gallery halls. The tsunami that was to become Leomania came crashing down on him.

Leonardo then accepted a small, self-mirroring role as a

> Long an art lover, he decided to visit the Louvre in Paris. But he had to leave that venerable art institution because he was spotted by packs of young girls who chased him through gallery halls.

spoiled Hollywood teen idol in Woody Allen's *Celebrity*, but otherwise he waited for the wave to pass.

Meanwhile, in trying to find some order in a chaotic life, he fueled the gossip by joining his friends in a highly publicized jet-setting high-life that extended from the trendy clubs of L.A. to seedy bars in Thailand. He was photographed with a succession of beautiful women on his arm, mostly model Kristen Zang on and off for about three years. His friends gave him some feeling of stability. The omnivorous media had dubbed them the "pussy posse," much to Leonardo's stated horror. "That is the most terribly degrading term for women I've ever heard, and I've never used that word in my life," he offered in his own behalf. He found some relief blowing off steam in the kind of exuberant lifestyle that was fodder to the circling sharks of the press. Although sometimes the numbers bloated up to hundreds of hangers-on, the core of his gang of good ol' boys included Tobey Maguire, Lukas Haas, Mark Wahlberg, alternative movie director Harmony Korine and magician David Blaine. (Although by 2002, Blaine had had enough. "He was definitely a great friend, and we definitely used to have a lot of fun together," Blaine told *Rolling Stone*. "But I don't love always being referred to as a friend of Leo's. It's like you have to have your own identity.")

Sometimes the high jinks turned nasty. In 1999, Leo and his gang were sued by one Roger Wilson, the (then) boyfriend of actress Elizabeth Berkley (*Showgirls*). Wilson charged that DiCaprio telephoned his girlfriend repeatedly trying to force his unwanted attentions on her. Wilson says he got fed up and came after the star. After the supposed altercation, Wilson alleged that he had "a broken larynx and other injuries," and sued for

> **He found some relief blowing off steam in the kind of exuberant lifestyle that was fodder to the circling sharks of the press.**

Celebrity (1998)

$45 million. Leonardo appeared at the trial in a sworn (but taped) deposition stating that he had no romantic interest in Miss Berkley and that he did not egg his friends on in the alleged beating. The court obviously believed Leo's story. The proceedings dragged on until September 2004 when the presiding judge threw it out for lack of evidence.

Then there were the perks that come with fame and lots of money. In 1998, Leonardo rented a waterfront mansion in trendy South Beach in Miami and flew in a dozen friends to celebrate New Year's Eve with him. He loaded the place with caviar, smoked oysters and expensive champagne. In Italy while making *Gangs of New York*, he partied so loudly and so often at his hotel that co-star Daniel Day-Lewis moved out to get some peace.

Despite Leo's protestations of just wanting to have fun, the frustration of his life and the dissolution of his lifestyle began to show. Shots of him appeared with a double chin and a stomach that was beginning to hang over his belt. His womanizing was legendary even if mostly created by the press, but he was a frequent guest at Hugh Hefner's Playboy Mansion. He was asked over and over again about the possibility of any permanent relationship, and he always replied, "I have no significant other at the moment, and I'm not looking for a serious relationship right now. I want to concentrate on my career."

In 1997, he finally moved out of his mother's home and into his own digs. He still maintains the most cordial relationships with his parents, frequently flying them to his various shoots worldwide.

Through it all, Leonardo has struggled to keep it real in a surreal world. His friends have stood by him—most of them refusing to speak about him to the press. They maintained that during the roller-coaster ride after *Titanic*, the actor continued to be just "Leo from the 'hood." That's the way the hard-nosed Hollywood producer of *Gangs of New York* Harvey Weinstein sees him.

When the two visited the Cannes Film Festival to promote the film, Weinstein told the press, "He's the biggest star I've ever dealt with, and he's such a good kid. The security around him is awesome—police with nightsticks, everybody so hyper, wary and juiced up—but he is the same charming boy I've always known him to be. And he did everything he promised. He stopped and talked to the press and posed, and they all got what they wanted. I don't think that even now he fully comprehends how and why *Titanic* changed his life so drastically. He's appreciative and tries to keep a sense of humor. But this madness is not him at all."

Perhaps to put some of Leo's story in context, one might go to writer/actor Edward Burns' comment to the *New York Times*. "If this sort of stuff bothers [an actor] so much you should go do regional theater. Go do Chekov in Iowa. No paparazzi will be following you."

chapter 10

No!
I shall not die today.

—Richard (Leonardo DiCaprio) telling the story of his fight with a shark in *The Beach*.

By 1999, the time had come for Leonardo DiCaprio to restart his career. His choice seemed to be the right one at the time. He wanted a role to bring back the edge to his character—something that the heartthrob status of *Titanic* had robbed him of—a role that would challenge him as an actor and return him to his glory days of critical credibility. He was hurting from another first for the actor—the mixed-to-bad reviews he had received for *The Man in the Iron Mask* and *Celebrity*. "I've gone to being the Antichrist," he groused to the *New York Times*.

"After *Romeo + Juliet* and *Titanic*, I was determined not to play another doomed lover. When I read *The Beach*, I knew I'd found a character I wanted to play. He's neither a hero nor a villain. He's just searching for paradise."

Writer/director Danny Boyle was just coming off *Trainspotting*, a searing but darkly humorous view of the life of a group of British heroin addicts. The film created a lot of buzz if not a lot of box office. It also made a star of its lead actor, Ewan McGregor.

But apparently not a big enough star. McGregor was set to play the lead in Boyle's movie adaptation of Alex Garland's cult novel, but when Leonardo showed an interest in the project, so did the big investors. Suddenly, the budget shot into the stratosphere, the interloper was offered his biggest paycheck yet ($20 million), and McGregor was out. (The incident caused a bitter rift between long-time friends Boyle and McGregor that was not patched up until 2003.)

In *The Beach*, DiCaprio plays Richard, a footloose young adventurer rambling around Thailand on his way to somewhere else. In Bangkok, he

The Beach (2000)

meets a crazed man who calls himself Daffy Duck. The obviously deranged fellow gives Richard a map of a secret isle that has been turned into a hippie-like paradise for those who have the courage to find it. Daffy then kills himself so, of course, Richard goes looking for the fabled isle. He takes a couple of equally free-spirited French strangers with him, and after much difficulty and a run-in with some ruthless drug farmers who also inhabit the island, they become part of the ragtag commune that has found its own brand of earthly heaven on this latter-day Bali Hai.

But things go terribly wrong—a sexual roundelay, shark attacks, death and a furious battle with the local marijuana growers. Eventually, Richard goes native in the jungle, and the movie evolves from *The Blue Lagoon* to *Lord of the Flies* and then just wanders off to get lost in its own tangled *Heart of Darkness* story.

During the filming, the participants were often in considerable danger. One day, while Boyle was shooting on a calm ocean, eight-foot waves arose out of nowhere and washed 15 crew members and performers out to sea. The boats were swamped, and everyone, including Leonardo, had to leap into the turbulent seas. "I was raised in Venice Beach [in Los Angeles], which is by the sea. I'm a good swimmer, and I understand waves," Leonardo told the *Calgary Sun*'s Louis B. Hobson. "I knew that in cases like this, you don't swim for shore but rather drift farther out to sea. I also knew I could float. If you swim back, the waves will just carry you out again, and you've wasted all that energy. I could see some people were panicking, and so I went to their aid." Boyle backed up the star, noting that Leo did the best he could to calm the terrified crew members. Later, boats dispatched from the shore picked them up. "I was convinced people were going to die," shivers Boyle. "It was a chilling experience, but Leo was cool about it. He knew he wouldn't die. Unfortunately, one of the divers sold the story to the newspapers. It angered all of us, especially Leo,

> One day, while Boyle was shooting on a calm ocean, eight-foot waves arose out of nowhere and washed 15 crew members and performers out to sea.

in the way it was reported. They either made it sound as if Leo single-handedly saved everyone or reported it so flippantly that it diminished the seriousness of what happened that day."

But the jellyfish sting Leonardo suffered during the shoot couldn't have been any more painful than the reception the film received. Even Leo's faithful audience wasn't interested in coming along with him as he searched for earthly paradise. Critics were almost unanimous in their condemnation of the film and the star's performance. "All you can think is how hard he is trying to act," complained the *Dallas Morning News*. "How did DiCaprio come to this lowly state after turning in spellbinding performances [in other films]?" The Knight Ridder News Service sourly observed, "His nonstop sulk helped sink a movie that would have capsized even without him."

Unfortunately, around the same time, a past piece of bad judgment was rising from murky waters. Years earlier, the actor had appeared gratis in a short black-and-white film, *Don's Plum*, shot by his friend R.D. Robb. The experimental movie, mostly improvised and shot over six days, also featured his pals Tobey Maguire and Kevin Connolly. The condition was that the film never be released as a feature. Leo played a wife-beating drug addict. *Don's Plum* was filled with pithy street language and ugly situations, the sort of images that the newly minted star didn't want to share with his fans. But with Leo's huge popularity, Robb decided to go back to the editing room, create a full-length feature by splicing in the outtakes and release it to some prestigious film festivals on its way to the big screen. This created a fractious situation as Leonardo tried to prevent the film from being released, and Robb countered with a legal suit against him to the tune of $10 million. *Don's Plum* was finally released internationally in 2001 to scathing reviews. Unable to find a distributor with enough interest to back it, the film has never seen general release in North America.

> "All you can think is how hard he is trying to act," complained the **Dallas Morning News**. "How did DiCaprio come to this lowly state after turning in spellbinding performances [in other films]?"

The Beach (2000)

Meanwhile, Leonardo, following the fictional road traveled by Bill Murray in Sophia Coppola's film *Lost in Translation*, then journeyed to Japan to make a commercial to be seen only in that country. Leo plays a classic Hollywood detective dressed in stylish black who bursts into a trendy bar, sees the bad guy and lays him out with one punch. A timid waiter approaches and asks, "Who is paying the bill, sir?" Leonardo barks out, "Orico card. Okay?" His appearance lasted about 15 seconds; he was paid $4 million.

The actor then created something of a stir when he apparently became interested in playing the lead in a film based on Bret Easton Ellis' controversial book, *American Psycho*. The tome is a brutal probe into the lifestyle of a psychopathic, self-obsessed yuppie killer of young women. Feminist groups attacked the publication for its graphic depictions of the murder of young females with such vigor that giant publisher Simon and Schuster dropped the title from its list. It was picked up and released by Vintage, a paperback imprint of Random House, and it sold modestly. Rumors began at the Cannes Film Festival that Leonardo had accepted the role and would be paid a jaw-dropping $21 million dollars by the small Canadian independent movie company Lion's Gate. The subsequent media tumult, which extended to a headline in the *Los Angeles Times*, cooled only when Leonardo's people stated the actor had never accepted the role in the first place. Later, the film was made and released in 2000 to little attention and even less box office starring the latest Batman, British actor Christian Bale.

Meanwhile, Leonardo moved on. While *American Psycho* struggled to find its audience, he was slated to star in films for two directors recognized as being among the best at their craft in the world—Martin Scorsese and Steven Spielberg.

chapter 11

I took the father. Now, I'll take the son.

—Bill "the Butcher" Cutting (Daniel Day-Lewis)
from *Gangs of New York*.

"I heard about this project when I was 16—the story of a young Irish immigrant in the 1800s who is placed in the center of the biggest urban riot in the world. I was so determined to do this project with him [director Martin Scorsese] that I actually changed agencies when I was 17 in order to be in closer contact." Leonardo DiCaprio speaking about his first intimations of Scorsese's dream film, *Gangs of New York*.

"It was when I learned that Marty had seen every movie ever made until the 1980s—I was working with a true visionary, someone who can masterfully assemble all the hidden mechanisms that make a movie operate with seamless reality and dramatic force."

After many fits, starts and dalliances with films ranging from *American Psycho* to the western *All the Pretty Horses*, Leonardo was clearly restless. One of the actor's agents, Rick Yorn, thought that what the young actor needed was the discipline of a project helmed by a strong-willed, world-class director. At that moment, Scorsese was promoting the film he had dreamed of making for a quarter of a century—the one that had caught Leo's attention so many years before. No one was much interested until Hollywood power broker Michael Ovitz was invited to a meeting where Scorsese was pitching his vision for *Gangs of New York*. He stated "I have just one thing to say to you Marty: Leonardo DiCaprio."

Mr. DiCaprio, meet Mr. Scorsese.

Yorn arranged the introduction. Surprisingly, the bright, if somewhat unfocused actor and the seasoned director hit it off right away. Like most people in the business, DiCaprio venerated Scorsese for his immense knowledge of the movies as well as for his string of near-mythic films ranging from *Mean Streets* and *Raging Bull* to *Goodfellas* and *Casino*. Like DiCaprio, Scorsese was a street kid, if from the other side of the continent. The actor knew the director could be maddeningly and frustratingly slow and demanding on set, but he respected Martin's strength and sure knowledge of filmmaking. Those who attended the meeting later reported that Leo was no pushover, passionately debating character, dialogue and plot points with Scorsese.

Leonardo committed to the project on the night he left Los Angeles to start *The Beach*. During the next 18 months, both would regret the decision, although Leonardo commented in Scorsese's book on the making of *Gangs of New York*, "Despite our original operatic arguments about the story [and my character], I have to say that I will truly never forget our first meetings. It was when I learned that Marty had seen every movie ever made until the 1980s—I was working with a true visionary, someone who can masterfully assemble all the hidden mechanisms that make a movie operate with seamless reality and dramatic force."

As for Scorsese, he saw DiCaprio as much more than a money magnet. The director told an interviewer for the Knight Ridder News Service in 1999, "He's the best young actor around. When you look over his entire body of work, you see his power. I always notice an actor's eyes. Leo's got fire in his eyes." He developed his thesis to the **London Standard** that same year, "I feel DiCaprio is on the level of De Niro, Pacino or Hoffman, no doubt about it."

Scorsese's quest to film *Gangs of New York* had epic and operatic elements all its own. Growing up in New York's Little Italy, the future director had heard of tales of great street battles between Catholic Irish immigrants and American-born Protestant gangs who felt they were the only true Americans. In 1970, Scorsese asked his friend, film critic/screenwriter Jay Cocks, to write a treatment. The project simmered on a back burner while various backers wrestled with a story whose commercial prospects seemed iffy. In 1977, Scorsese took out an ad in the Hollywood trade papers stating that he was embarking on the film, but the violent nature of the subject matter and the daunting budget demanded by a period film proved too much for the studios and again the money disappeared like the morning fog on a Malibu Beach.

The director was blindsided by the conundrum his distinguished career had left him. He was one of the most highly regarded auteurs in the world, but his much-lauded films just didn't make a lot of money. His only movie to generate big box office returns was a film he made to show he could produce a commercial hit—*Cape Fear*. He had developed a reputation for striking a budget, getting the money and then ignoring it while he created "art." The big studios were afraid of what they saw as arrogance and artistic indulgence and feared being left with the tab when it was all over.

And, in truth, a violent 19th-century period piece about a forgotten time in New York's history was not one to inspire much faith for huge box office returns. Besides, modern-day New York looked nothing like it did in those years, and so a whole new lower Manhattan would have to be built somewhere. In addition, the movie mavens couldn't come to grips with just what kind of a film it would be.

Scorsese insisted it was not a period gangster movie like his great artistic successes but a sort of urban western. It's easy to see why the idea appealed to him so much. These were the muddy roadways that Scorsese would return to time and again throughout his distinguished career in films like *Goodfellas* and *Taxi Driver*. In his screenplay was lived out an elemental story of love and revenge set in a roiling context that was to shape the New York that Scorsese returned to again and again in his movies.

> **For many years, Gangs of New York continued to make the circles of the studios gaining the reputation as an "unmakable" film. Then along came Leonardo with his box office clout and huge fan base, who was determined he would not devote his career to the hysterical bubble gummers spawned by Titanic, demanding that his agents find edgy, quirky roles. And projects made by distinguished directors.**

Mr. Scorsese, meet Mr. Weinstein.

Riding to the rescue of Scorsese's stalled vision came an unlikely savior. Harvey Weinstein is the blunt-spoken, roly-poly co-head (with his brother) of the Miramax Film Corporation—a company best known for picking up foreign art films and brilliantly marketing them to large audiences. But Weinstein had bigger ambitions and wanted to produce his own films. Miramax came up with most of the money (the budget was set at $85 million), but it also brought Harvey along. Harvey had his own ideas and hated self-indulgent filmmaking.

The battles between the free-spending director and the brusque, no-nonsense money man were apparently of epic proportions. One example was when Weinstein refused to allow a nearly full-size cathedral to be built on the huge set in Rome's legendary Cinecitta Studios. The set, designed by Dante Ferretti, was already a meticulous recreation of mid-19th-century New York and sprawled over several city blocks. Sagging, jumbled tenements lined cobblestoned and garbage-strewn streets, while ragged laundry hung from upper windows. At the end of the street, two tall sailing ships, built to scale, were moored at a dock.

Because of the insecurity of the filmmakers, the tension on set and the public's fascination with the movie's stars, security was tight. Weinstein allowed only George Lucas and Tom Cruise to visit his creation. But Weinstein lived to regret even that decision. Cruise sided with Scorsese on the need for the cathedral. Weinstein sighed and reached for his wallet. "Tom's very persuasive," he shrugged later. From then on, the cathedral was known as St. Thomas after its patron saint and champion.

With Leonardo firmly in place, Scorsese set out to find a co-star. He had hoped his close personal friend and acting muse Robert De Niro would take the part of Leonardo's nemesis in the film, "Bill the Butcher." But when the performer learned that filming the behemoth would take many months and that it would be shot a long way from his home in New York, he declined the role. Scorsese's next choice was the actor who had given him a controlled and brilliant performance in his *The Age of Innocence*—Oscar winner (*My Left Foot*) Daniel Day-Lewis. But Day-Lewis had decided to change careers, having signed on as an apprentice shoemaker in Florence.

Mr. Day-Lewis, meet Mr. DiCaprio.

Scorsese managed to persuade the eccentric actor to fly to New York where he marshaled his secret weapon: Leonardo DiCaprio. By this time Leo was consulting regularly on the script. The two actors hit it off immediately and began deep discussions on the characters they were to play. Leonardo's commitment and charm impressed the would-be cobbler, and after several meetings, Day-Lewis signed on. When Cameron Diaz agreed to appear as the love interest, the box office names on the marquee were complete.

Gangs of New York (2002)

After 25 years of waiting, Scorsese and his young star passed through the gates of Cinecitta Studios in September 2000 and began shooting the movie the director had imagined for all those years "about the city I love and how it recreated itself."

Gangs of New York is set in the mid-1800s in the unimaginable squalor of a section of lower Manhattan, in a powder keg known as the Five Points. The story revolves around a young boy, Amsterdam Vallon (DiCaprio). His father (Liam Neeson) is called "the Priest" and is the leader of the Irish gang. As the film begins, we see the gang sharpening knives, praying before a cross and then moving into the street to confront the "Nativists" led by William Cutting (Day-Lewis), known as "Bill the Butcher." Bill is the head of the fiercely anti-immigrant faction and a key to the unruly power structure of the time. After a ferocious and bloody battle, Amsterdam sees his father carved up by Bill before his eyes.

Fifteen years later, Amsterdam returns from "the house of refuge," a reformatory for young criminals. He conceals his identity, waiting for the moment that he can have his revenge on Bill. However, in spite of himself, he is drawn into the orbit of the charismatic older man, going so far as to become a member of Bill's gang. The two grow so close that it doesn't seem to bother Bill when Amsterdam takes up with Bill's old flame Jenny (Diaz), a winsome pickpocket and sometime prostitute who tries to operate independently of the

> "I've always felt that it was preferable to allow that confrontation. When it happens, it should take place in such a way that you don't know too much about each other. Surprise is always the best thing."

gangs. The story tells of the great draft riots of 1863, when New Yorkers violently protested an effort to conscript them into what they saw as Mr. Lincoln's war against the South. After four days of carnage, which nearly burned the city to the ground, the government called in the army, which violently put down the riot, creating the most dramatic episode of urban unrest in American history. Inevitably, Bill and Amsterdam meet in a final confrontation.

As the battle over money (Weinstein) and creative expression (Scorsese) raged about them, the actors disappeared into their roles. Day-Lewis grew even more impressed with DiCaprio. "We had everything we could wish for in a working relationship," he enthusiastically observed at the end of filming. The two didn't socialize offscreen much because, said the actor, "We didn't have time. I think we both understood implicitly that the nature of the collision between us required that we approach each other, but we keep a distance as well. On film shoots there's always a lot of interesting people around, and it sometimes alleviates the sense of isolation you feel. I think there's something dangerous about that. I've always felt that it was preferable to allow that confrontation. When it happens, it should take place in such a way that you don't know too much about each other. Surprise is always the best thing."

Day-Lewis stayed in character throughout much of the shoot, literally terrifying some of the supporting players.

> It's a good thing the two stars got along. In an echo of his experience with Robert De Niro in **This Boy's Life**, DiCaprio broke Day-Lewis' nose in a particularly violent confrontation. Day-Lewis, with a bloody nose, kept filming until the scene was done.

For his part, Leonardo worked hard to create a believable character. He poured over the handwritten journal of a young man who spent his entire youth in a reform school. He spent the 11 months it took to get the project rolling bulking up, learning various street-fighting techniques as well as how to throw a knife.

Cameron Diaz commented to *Cosmopolitan Magazine*, "You wouldn't recognize Leonardo. He's a man now. He has really built himself up and is quite a presence." The two really threw themselves into their big raunchy and violent love scene. "We basically beat the shit out of each other for the day. But it was a lot of fun. At one point, it became a test of stamina, like who was going to endure it, who was going to flail about the longest without have a compete coronary."

Since the set was locked up so tightly, the press circled like vultures trying to pick up any choice scrap of meat. Newspapers duly reported that Leonardo's high life resulted in his ballooning to pudgy proportions, and he had to be put on a strict diet by Harvey Weinstein. "Not true," observed *Variety* editor Peter Bart, who was allowed to visit the set and reported that Leo was "thin as a rod." A report that seems to have a little more grist to it (mostly because it was recorded by an enterprising sound technician) was a 10-minute dressing down the frustrated director gave his star on set in front of everyone. According to the report, DiCaprio appeared late on set one morning with a hangover and not knowing his lines. With some excisions, Scorsese's rant runs like this:

Scorsese: "Alright Mr. Partyboy, Mr. King of the World, Mr. I Don't Give a Shit About Anybody Else! Don't roll your eyes at me. Do you think Robert De Niro keeps everybody waiting?"

DiCaprio: "Yeah…but…"

Scorsese: "You make me sick. You make everybody sick. You make me violently ill. Do you think Willem Dafoe enjoyed spending 12 days nailed to a cross for *The Last Temptation*? You don't think he would have rather been out doing cocaine and ecstasy? Of course, he

> "You wouldn't recognize Leonardo. He's a man now. He has really built himself up and is quite a presence."

would have. But he was on the set every day. You can't even show up for your kissing scene with Cameron Diaz, you little pussy. What's the matter, don't you like girls?"

DiCaprio: " I do like girls, but…"

Scorsese: "Who the hell doesn't want to kiss Cameron Diaz? Did you do this to James Cameron? Hell no! If you had, he'd have thrown you off the boat. You know what I'm going to do with you, you little turd. Forget the kissing scene. Forget Cameron Diaz. We're going to the wharf set to film our bare-knuckle boxing scene. You versus Oscar De La Hoya as an Italian fighter. I'm going to give your stunt double the afternoon off, so you're going to film the scene yourself, you little piece of…"

> You get the idea… The story goes on that when Scorsese cooled down, he made his high-priced star apologize to the entire cast and crew. Whether it happened or not, it makes interesting reading. Leonardo's well-oiled PR machine issued an immediate disclaimer, stating that the event never happened.

The film went way over budget and schedule. Finally, DiCaprio and Scorsese themselves came up with $7 million of their own to cover the overages.

The stars and the impressive supporting cast, which included Oscar winner Jim Broadbent (*Moulin Rouge*), Brendon Gleeson (*Troy*), John C. Reilly (*Chicago*) and Henry Thomas (*Legends of the Fall*), worked hard for their driving taskmaster, but as one executive observed, "Marty's problem is that he's shooting with a cold script. He has to build in emotion with his actors."

The film opened just before Christmas 2002, and while some reviewers declared it to be a masterpiece, many more were less impressed. Despite its length (2 hours and 45 minutes), it seemed too short. Somewhere, Scorsese probably has a three-hour plus director's cut that develops his themes to their logical conclusions—the logic that eluded the version that was released. The director steadfastly refused to blame Weinstein for the film's truncated feel, but the comment from insiders was that Weinstein forced the director to chop his opus into a more audience- (and exhibitor-) friendly length. As it stands, *Gangs of New York* cries out for more plot and character development. Characters come and go, changing completely for little apparent reason. Diaz's Jenny starts off as a fascinating and feisty creation and then morphs into your basic ingenue. After the spectacular draft riots of 1863, the final face-off between Amsterdam and Bill the Butcher is anticlimactic. Many of the big events of the final half-hour, such as the conscription of the locals to fight in the American Civil War by a distant federal government, seem to come out of nowhere.

Leonardo did not fare well either. After a strong beginning, the movie begins to play to the actor's weaknesses rather than his strengths. Poor Leo is left to dourly watch the movie unfold around him behind a grubby little chin beard and a perpetual scowl. His character becomes rather a conventional fellow requiring naturalism and a minimalist approach. He is a time bomb planted in "Bill the Butcher's" life and spends much of the film hiding his feelings from everyone.

Meanwhile, Day-Lewis unleashes one of the most overpowering and impressive (although really weird) performances in recent movie history. Sounding more foreign than many of the immigrants, he pronounces his words with a precise, otherworldly speech pattern. He screws his face up, and under his handlebar mustache shaking with emotion, his lips curl like a villain from an old

> Leonardo did not fare well either. After a strong beginning, the movie begins to play to the actor's weaknesses rather than his strengths.

melodrama. One minute he's juggling his cleaver while carving a pig into chops and the next he's striding through the Five Points, intently bent forward. In his stovepipe hat, long maroon waistcoat and yellow trousers, you can't take your eyes off him. It's an astounding, Oscar-friendly, scene-chewing performance that blows his co-star out of the water.

> **The battle about the relative merits *Gangs of New York* will probably continue in film studies programs at universities for years to come. Perhaps some day Scorsese will return to the editing room and release his version of the film, and we'll see if it is more of a lasting masterpiece than the film that was released in 2002.**

Barely pausing to catch his breath, Leonardo moved on to work with another cinematic master, and this time it was a film designed to showcase both the boyish charm and talent that made the actor not only catnip at the box office but a performer of considerable scope and skill.

chapter 12

Ho! Ho! Ho! Well! Well! Well!
Now who's being stupid.

—Jack (Leonardo DiCaprio) to Rose (Kate Winslet)
on the deck of *Titanic*

Leonardo was in Rome making *Gangs of New York* when his cabal of advisors sent him a script taken from the bestseller, *Catch Me If You Can*, written two decades earlier by legendary scam artist Frank Abagnale Jr. The script had no director attached, but to Leonardo, caught in the mud, mire and behind-the-camera battles of his current shoot, the sunny, funny story of the agile Abagnale looked like a perfect change of pace.

The star was interested but not yet committed, so his people asked Leonardo to assemble a list of prospective directors he would consider for the film. He compiled his dream list but purposely left Steven Spielberg out. "I never put Steven on that list because I never imagined it would be a movie he was interested in."

But the great director found himself in a position similar to Leo's. He was just off the murky sci-fi thrillers *Artificial Intelligence: AI* and *Minority Report*. "I was in something of a dark place," admits Spielberg. He, too, was looking for a change of pace, something lighter.

The hot young writer/director Gore Verbinsky, who went on to make the creepy film *The Ring* and followed that with *Pirates of the Caribbean: The Curse of the Black Pearl*, was selected as the director of the piece, and Spielberg, who also read the script and loved it, came on as producer. "I was like the many people who fell under the seductive influence of the real Frank William Abagnale Jr. just through the book," offered Spielberg. "And when you meet him, you understand in a second how he could pull the wool over your

Catch Me If You Can (2002)

eyes and convince you that he was a doctor or a lawyer. Personally, I've always loved movies about sensational rogues, like the Newman-Redford classics *Butch Cassidy and the Sundance Kid* and *The Sting*. They were breaking the law, but you loved them for their moxie."

As events subsequently developed, Verbinsky was forced to drop out because of previous commitments when Leonardo was summoned back to Rome to film some pick-up scenes for Scorsese, and much to the actor's delight, Spielberg decided to take over the reins. "I enjoy that whiplash sensation of going from *Jurassic Park* to *Schindler's List* and now from *Minority Report* to *Catch Me If You Can*. Selfishly, it was also an opportunity to work with a young actor I've always admired."

> **So the actor who had aged sufficiently to believably lead a vicious gang war in Gangs of New York found himself a kid again, playing a character 11 years younger than himself.**

Abagnale published his memoirs in 1980. The real-life, cat-and-mouse thriller seemed like a natural for the movies, but no one could come up with a treatment that worked, and so it bounced from studio to studio for more than 20 years.

The film tracks the outrageous adventures of a 16-year-old suffering through the divorce of his beloved parents. Running away from his unfaithful mother and crumbling father (Christopher Walken inventively cast against type), he sets out to create a life for himself. Blessed with

> **"I enjoy that whiplash sensation of going from Jurassic Park to Schindler's List and now from Minority Report to Catch Me If You Can. Selfishly, it was also an opportunity to work with a young actor I've always admired."**

the classical con man's suavity, a diabolically brilliant mind and an ability to think fast on his feet, he creates several lives. Both the film and the book suggest that the motivation behind his schemes was to bring his parents back together and pay back the huge debt in back taxes his father's own suspect schemes had incurred.

Commented Abagnale, "It begins with my parent's divorce and its dramatic effect on me. I ran away and suddenly found myself a teenager alone in the world. I had to grow up very quickly and become very creative in order to survive. But what started out as survival became a game. I asked myself, 'Could I get away with that?' Then there was the satisfaction of actually getting away with it. The more I got away with, the more of a game it became—a game I knew I would ultimately lose, but a game I was going to have fun playing until I did."

> **The story takes place in the '60s—a much more innocent time, one more conducive to a charismatic con man pulling off his inventive scams. A man in uniform was still a figure to be admired. "It was a time of tremendous trust, when you never locked your doors but felt safe," observed Spielberg.**

Abagnale may have only been 16, but he looked and carried himself as a considerably older person. He commandeered the uniform of a Pan Am pilot and started cashing his homemade but impressive, real-looking checks at banks all over New York. He worked out an elaborate scheme that gave him weeks before the offending slips were processed and the authorities came looking for the money. Before he was tracked down, he had cashed about $2.5 million worth of fraudulent checks while posing as a pilot, an international spy, a doctor and a lawyer. Abagnale was so bright, in fact, that he passed the Louisiana Bar exam after two weeks of study.

Abagnale eventually caught the eye of implacable FBI agent Carl Hanratty (Tom Hanks in a role originally meant for *The Soprano*'s James Gandolfini), a stoic sort of fellow with no life, who makes it his personal quest to capture the illusive paperhanger. Says Hanks of his character's obsession with the young scam artist, "Carl is so impressed with the style and panache of his quarry that he's doubly astounded to discover how young he is. Carl suddenly realizes that he's just a kid, incredibly gifted, but ultimately a child, who is in the midst of an adventure that is bigger than he is. Carl comes to feel almost protective of Frank. He treats him like a criminal—he is going to send him to jail—but at end of the day, he sees a fragile human being who is worth trying to redeem somehow."

After the experience of *Gangs of New York*, *Catch Me If You Can* was a happy experience for Leonardo. He respected Spielberg and loved working with Hanks. The feeling was mutual between the two actors. The ever-droll Hanks observed that working with Leonardo was like being Hooch in *Turner and Hooch* (referring to an earlier Hanks film—Hooch was an unlovable, slobbering lump of a dog). For his part, Leonardo told one interviewer, "Hanks is very much a role model for me because he is able to take whatever he does, whittle it down and refine the work. He has such a passion for the work and such exuberance, and I think, every day feels lucky to be there. Ironically, he is [one of] the most powerful and great actors in our business, but at the same time he feels lucky to be doing what he does. I certainly don't want to be cynical about what I do. He was a great example of how to retain all that even when in the upper echelons our business."

> After the experience of ***Gangs of New York, Catch Me If You Can*** was a happy experience for Leonardo. He respected Spielberg and loved working with Hanks. The feeling was mutual between the two actors.

The two actors had widely differing approaches to movie acting. Hanks felt he had nailed the obsessive nature of the FBI agent, and when he got a good take would want to move on. Leonardo, on the other hand, was seldom satisfied. "Leo has a very interesting process," Spielberg told

Newsweek in 2002. "He gets better with every take because he's very self-critical and gets very involved with his playbacks. I used to beg Tom in *Private Ryan*. I'd pull him over to the monitor, because he'd say 'Hey, boss, I felt good about that last take' and then walk away. I'd say, 'Tom, you've got to see this.' It's very hard to get him to the monitor, but Leo goes to the monitor like a bee to honey."

> Leonardo prepared for the role by spending time with Abagnale. He invited him to his Hollywood Hills home for a few days of observation and long conversations. Remembers Abagnale, "He followed me around the house with a notebook and a tape recorder asking me questions. I was so impressed at how seriously he takes his craft."

But somewhere along the way, the actor's art has to come into play. For one thing, despite the span in years between actor and character, DiCaprio—with a somewhat geeky haircut and a teenager's chipmunk awkwardness—was surprisingly able to recreate the adolescence he had left behind several movies ago. Commented the actor, "At a certain point you draw enough information from the person, and then you go off on your own and create the character and let that character have a life of its own. I didn't want to take away the spontaneity of young Frank going out into the world. I wanted the audience to be carried along with him on his journey to self-discovery, to see the sparkle in his eye the first time he sees an airline pilot being treated like royalty, or to watch his first mistakes as a pilot or lawyer. I didn't want to be too perfect because I believe Frank gets by more on his personality and charm and his ability to misdirect, rather than being perfect at impersonating people. I think that has a lot of do with the ego of this cocky kid who thinks he can defy anyone, including the FBI. And, in fact, does."

LEO FAN FACT

Leonardo was sick for much of the shooting of *Catch Me If You Can*. Steven Spielberg told the *Hollywood Reporter*, "He got very sick with a chest cold and was not able to shake it off because he kept working. You can't shake off things when you are on set for 12 hours a day. Whenever he heard 'roll' he would rally and do amazing work then grab a Kleenex and go back to the trailer."

Leonardo probed deeper. "In my initial meetings with Frank, I asked, 'Besides putting on these costumes, did you ever put on an accent, put on a personality, become an actor trying to be somebody?' He was like, 'No. No. I was always myself. I never changed who I was. I just studied the profession.' I said, 'Well give me an example of you talking to Pan Am, forging a check.' Suddenly, and I think really unconsciously, he slipped into this southern drawl. I said, 'Do you know what you're doing?' He's like, 'No, I don't know what I just did.' 'You were speaking like you were from Texas!' 'No I wasn't,' he said. I said, 'Yes you were.' 'That's how I always talk when I'm a pilot.' It was so interesting because it was instinctual on his part. He was almost a great actor. The southern drawl, at the time, must have been the 'Voice of Authority' to him. He established in his mind that people would look at him differently if he had this Voice of Authority, you know, with NASA and everything like that. It was a very trustworthy sounding accent."

You don't have to look very hard at *Catch Me If You Can* to notice the genuine pleasure of everyone involved in the project. After the locked-down discipline of Scorsese's *Gangs of New York*, Spielberg was trying to capture the high-energy, roller-coaster thrill of Abagnale's life by moving fluidly and quickly from set-up to set-up. The director is noted for running a happy set where everyone is encouraged to have input into the filmmaking. Leonardo enthused, "He's so open-minded, not just to me as an actor but to people in every department. I think that is part of what makes him a great director. He brings out the best in you and gets everyone working like a well-oiled machine towards a common goal."

Leonardo's favorite scene is probably the most memorable image the film has left with audiences—the spectacle of his character striding through the Miami airport surrounded by bevies of adoring stewardesses—hidden in plain sight. Chuckles the star, "The FBI was teeming around the airport with an 8 x 10 of his face, and he knew that. It was almost like he was playing with the world around him, testing to see how far he could go. That's the art of the magician, when somebody does something that is so obvious that it couldn't be true."

Many of these comments come directly from interviews Leonardo gave on a junket shortly before the film was released. Junkets are the bane of many an actor's life. For several weeks, they are expected to dutifully make the rounds of the talk shows to beat the drum for their latest picture. But the real heavy lifting comes during the weekend when entertainment journalists are flown in from all over the world. The stars of the film are anchored in a single hotel room, and one after the other, reporters are ushered in. Imagine it: one stuffy room, a television crew with its lights and cameras and an unending stream of eager, young journalists all asking the same questions over and over again for their five minutes of glory with the star. Paul Newman on his first junket complained to me plaintively one long afternoon, "Don't you guys ever stop. You've been coming in all day. I'll never do this again. Is the end of the line in sight yet?" I didn't have the heart to tell him there was yet

> Junkets are the bane of many an actor's life. For several weeks, they are expected to dutifully make the rounds of the talk shows to beat the drum for their latest picture.

another whole room of us waiting. Jack Nicholson once gritted out, "I'd rather have red hot needles inserted into my eyeballs than ever go through that process."

And they don't get paid one extra cent for the time and effort.

So why is the notoriously press-shy Leonardo sitting in that small, overheated room at the end of a marathon four-day junket? Said the star, "I think it's important that the purpose of being out in the public eye for an actor is to promote a film. Other than charitable reasons there is no other point to it. Otherwise I think it's harder and harder over the course of time to believe you in roles, as an actor. They become so accustomed to who you are they don't buy into you in different situations. It's been my thought throughout—and it's ironic to say that because I am splashed all over the gossip columns. Not to my liking."

So how does he deal with it?

"I just don't deal with it is what I do. Who I am is spoken for up on the screen. I can't get on a podium and declare who I am or clarify every story written about me. It's a waste of time and a no-win battle." And in a comment, the new, more mature and responsible Leonardo is often heard saying nowadays, "I want my movies to speak for who I am."

Catch Me If You Can was released at Christmas 2002, one week after *Gangs of New York*. A frustrated Leonardo reportedly tried to get at least a month's breathing room between the two films, but the studios wanted that big Christmas audience for both releases. When he lost that battle, a resigned Leonardo sighed, "Well, people will get a look at two completely different characters, and that representation of me as an actor is a good thing."

Actually the two films have some surprising similarities between them. Both characters are loving sons out to avenge their presumably wronged fathers. As a young boy, Amsterdam (*Gangs of New York*) watched his father slashed to death by the gangs of Nativists led by Bill the Butcher. As a worshipful teenager, Frank Abagnale was devastated by his parents' divorce and driven into his wildly inventive schemes as he watched his father's shaky financial gambles crumble. The inspired grifter strove to make as much money as he could so that he might help his father realize his relatively small-scale dreams. Inevitably, both Frank and Amsterdam find surrogate fathers who would also become their nemeses.

The warm glow of *Catch Me If You Can* and its ingratiating characters caught the public's fancy and became an immediate hit, going on to earn over $250 million at the box office even before it was released to DVD. John Williams' score and Walken's conflicted father were nominated for Academy Awards. Leo won a nomination for a Golden Globe.

Throughout it all Leonardo still remembers who buys the tickets, and he holds his fans in high regard. He was apparently quite stunned when 2000 British fans turned up on a freezing winter night to greet him for the premiere of the film. He immediately went into the crowd of well wishers, shaking hands and giving autographs.

There is continuing talk of turning the movie into a Broadway musical— Steven Sondheim has been approached to write the lyrics.

Carl Hanratty did capture Frank Abagnale Jr. in France and sent him off to jail. Abagnale served some of his time but was released early so that he could use his skills as an FBI expert in tracking down other con artists. He has since become a millionaire as a consultant to major corporations, helping to design programs that can't be cracked by white-collar criminals.

As for Leo, he returned to the fold of an earlier mentor to help him re-create on film one of the most fascinating Americans of the 20th century.

chapter 13

I'm not a paranoid millionaire. Goddammit, I'm a billionaire.

–Howard Hughes.

Leonardo DiCaprio leaped at the chance to play Howard Hughes on the screen, saying, "He pushed every environment around him to its utter extremes. He was so driven. He was a pioneer in the world of aviation. He was a huge director in Hollywood. He was a womanizer; he was a germophobe; and he was obsessive-compulsive."

The story of maverick industrialist/movie-maker Howard Hughes is the stuff of legends and another one of those projects that simmered on Hollywood's back burner for decades until suddenly everyone had a Howard Hughes project. For many years, Warren Beatty tried to get his own version of the mythic aviator's life off the ground but couldn't find backing and then grew too old to play the dynamic young Hughes. Johnny Depp fronted one project backed by his *From Hell* directors, the Hughes brothers (no relation to Howard). Other visions of the story came from actor Edward Norton (*Fight Club*) and director Milos Forman (*Amadeus*). John Travolta, a well-known flyer, was rumored to have purchased one of Hughes' own aircraft to put himself on an inside track, and Nicholas Cage, with director Brian DePalma (*Carrie* and *Snake Eyes*) in tow, took flying lessons to make himself more Howard-friendly. Others mentioned for the role were John Cusack and George Clooney. But the biggest

> Leonardo DiCaprio leaped at the chance to play Howard Hughes on the screen...

competition came from Jim Carrey (*Ace Ventura*) with Chris Nolan (*Memento*) onboard to write and direct.

What excited Leonardo was that here was a film that focused in on Hughes' colorful earlier life and not the dirty, paranoid recluse he was to become. Leonardo describes Hughes in those later years as "the hairy wolf-man that sat up in his suite and overlooked the lights of Vegas." No, Leonardo would play the young devil-may-care adventurer who pushed the limits while trying to cope with the developing obsessive-compulsive behavior that was to consume him. (OCD had yet to be diagnosed and given a name.)

The director of Leonardo's particular take on the story was to be Michael Mann (*Heat* and *The Last of the Mohicans*), using a screenplay penned by John Logan (*Gladiator* and *Star Trek: Nemesis*). But Mann had just completed two reality-based biographical films, *The Outsider* and *Ali*, and tired of biopics, he decided to bow out as director to concentrate on other projects. And so, while staying on as producer, he turned his script and his movie over to the man who had inspired a whole generation of young filmmakers—Martin Scorsese.

Scorsese received the script while he was still working on *Gangs of New York* in Rome. A notorious non-flyer himself, he nevertheless grabbed the opportunity to film the life of this enigmatic giant of the skies. It not only featured DiCaprio, who obviously impressed the auteur during their current shoot together, but the director, who was something of an obsessive himself, harbored a long-time fascination with Hughes. One of Scorsese's favorite films was 1930's *Hell's Angels*, which was written and directed by the young Hughes.

> No, Leonardo would play the young devil-may-care adventurer who pushed the limits while trying to cope with the developing obsessive-compulsive behavior that was to consume him.

"I wanted to express the obsession with speed," says Scorsese, recalling how he had reacted to the script. "Always going faster, doing five films at once…seeing a thousand women at once. This voracious appetite for speed, this is what interested me in the picture, because the bottom line, underneath it all, he's destroying himself ultimately."

Howard Hughes inherited the Hughes Tool Company from his father at the age of 19. The senior Hughes had invented an innovative drill bit that is still used in the oil industry. Seemingly by ignoring basic capitalistic principals, Howard and the company continued to flourish, making him one of the richest men in the world and leaving him a great deal of time to pursue what he really wanted to do—make movies, bed some of the loveliest starlets of the '30s and '40s, fly his own personally designed aircraft, and later, move into the murky world of international espionage.

> **Hughes' early Hollywood career as a director and producer was impressive. He brought to the screen such classics as *The Front Page*, *Flying Leathernecks* and the controversial *Scarface*, making stars of Jean Harlow in *Hell's Angels* and Edward G. Robinson in *Scarface* (the 1932 version, which was a loose account of the life of Al Capone).**

In his youth, Hughes was a dapper, handsome man with a pencil mustache. He had the aura of power and an air of mystery and adventure about him. An avid and daring pilot, he set several world records including one in 1938 for an around-the-world flight in just 91 hours. Not everything worked, however. He developed the H-1 Racer plane that crashed into a beet field during a test flight. He also crash-landed his experimental XF-11 on a Beverly Hills street, seriously injuring himself. Both events are chronicled in the film.

Among many others, he had romantic liaisons with Katherine Hepburn (Cate Blanchett in the film) and Ava Gardner (Kate

The Aviator (2004)

Beckinsale). An inveterate tinkerer, he also invented the engineering marvel of the half-cup bra to adequately showcase the independent front suspension of Jane Russell—star of his steamy western *The Outlaw*.

The Aviator moves on to show Hughes branching out into the aviation industry heading up TWA (Trans World Airlines), a company he inaugurated to compete with Pan Am's virtual monopoly on international flights. The film outlines Hughes' stormy relationship with the prickly New England-born Hepburn. Both were single-minded, and it was a union doomed from the beginning, but fiery while it lasted. Kate Beckinsale took the role of Ava Gardiner after Nicole Kidman became unavailable. It's an interesting piece of casting because Beckinsale is slim and willowy, while Gardiner was a voluptuous starlet.

> **Also, making cameo appearances are such '30s movie-town players as Jean Harlow, Hughes' teenage squeeze, Faith Domergue, MGM founder Louis B. Mayer and Spencer Tracy. Jude Law is featured as that other great babe magnet of the '30s, Errol Flynn.**

By the 1950s (after *The Aviator* ends), Hughes became increasingly unbalanced, finally hiding in plain sight in Las Vegas, Vancouver, Panama and other world centers. He died in 1976 in such a deteriorated physical condition that he had to be identified, for official purposes, by his fingerprints.

While the financial chess players were maneuvering around the board trying to find the money for the $100 million film, Leonardo was, as usual, deep into research on Hughes' mythic character. Besides the legendary "master of the skies" aspect, Leonardo had to chart his chaotic emotional life and the beginnings of his descent into phobia and physical disability. Somewhat like Orson Wells' *Citizen Kane*, Hughes was a visionary builder of things, but his people skills were somewhat lacking. Leonardo watched all the newsreel footage of Hughes' exploits during those years. He read numerous books and accounts of Hughes' life, trying to find and project the humanity of the man. It's hard to build up too much empathy for a difficult and demanding technological wizard (and serial womanizer), who could buy his way out of any problem that came up. Leonardo, displaying the obsessive side of his own character, immersed himself in the arcane details of the entrepreneur's life. He even visited Hughes' old girl friends, including the magnificently cantilevered Jane Russell. (Ms. Russell was impressed with Leonardo but later told a reporter that she thought the actor was not enough like Hughes physically. "You need a long, lanky fellow like Jimmy Stewart to play him," she commented)

Even Scorsese, used to working with such method actors as Robert De Niro, was surprised with what Leonardo brought to the set. "There are 'shape changers,'" waxed the director. "People who change shape. This comes from ancient folklore or sagas from the North where men change shape in battle. They'd become ferocious animals or something.... We found ourselves at certain points in the picture when Leo would walk on the set...it was Howard, or at least our version of Howard. I hadn't seen that for a long time." Harking back to his earlier comment that only on certain occasions does he completely become the character he is portraying in a film, Leonardo himself felt the pull of the charismatic and troubled Hughes. "There are moments when you're acting wherein something comes over you where you, all of a sudden, feel as if the entire set and the director aren't there. It's almost like a weird trance-like state you get in," he comments.

> We found ourselves at certain points in the picture when Leo would walk on the set...it was Howard, or at least our version of Howard.

Leo probed so deeply that he found himself gripped by the re-awakened mild case of the Obsessive-Compulsive Disorder he'd suffered from as a child. To prepare for a key scene where Hughes experiences a breakdown in a projection room, Leonardo went though seven hours of make-up every day. "[The sequence] took about two weeks of shooting," marvels Scorsese. "Every gesture you see there, every move of his body, even the blinking of his eyes, was worked on way in advance and ultimately on set." Leonardo demanded as many as 20 takes, "each one slightly different in terms of the intensity of the disorder, including a nervous cough, twitches, touching his knee. Soft version. Soft reading, stronger readings, stranger readings."

> "I found it heartbreaking," echoes co-star Cate Blanchett (Katherine Hepburn) upon finishing the scene where Hughes is finally overtaken by his madness. "Just hearing his voice through the door [of the screening room]. That's when I really knew that he'd been transported or that he'd journeyed somewhere that he had never been before, because there was not trace of Leo at all."

"He's a genius," agrees Kate Beckinsale (Ava Gardner). "I mean, I think he's amazing. [We shot a lot of scenes] toward the end of the movie where he's really breaking down. He's just extraordinary." Apparently, Hughes saw Gardner as something of a savior. "It's very much that he's asking her to marry him all the time. They are good friends. She's very supportive of him once he's sick. She tells him, 'You're a bit too crazy for me.'"

Leonardo retained his usual press clampdown as the shooting of the film began in Montreal on July 7, 2003, and moved to Los Angeles in September.

Despite the raging wildfires of that autumn in Los Angeles that destroyed several of the production's key sets, Scorsese dumbfounded his detractors by bringing in the film only one day late and (reportedly) on budget.

On its release, *The Aviator* was greeted by many critics as one of Scorsese's masterpieces, while others saw it as yet another ponderous attempt at big-budget myth making. But few critics (or audiences) found any fault with Leonardo DiCaprio's uncanny performance as he balances the flamboyant elements of Hughes' career with the growing paranoia of a man too frightened of germs to open a bathroom door. The actor does an entirely creditable job making Hughes larger than life so that the audience experiences a great sense of sadness at the dwindling of his light. Leo's performance in *The Aviator* fulfills the promise of his early films with the added understanding and maturity of a man entering his 30s.

You can't take your eyes off him.

chapter 14

My Heart Will Go On

–Song, sung by Celine Dion over credits of Titanic Lyrics: Will Jennings. Music: James Horner.

So, what is Leonardo DiCaprio really like?

It was much easier to get a fix on the young boy growing up in a less-than-desirable section of Los Angeles. Or the young actor who seemed to make all the right decisions and brought an impressive talent to bear on his choices.

But with the advent of his outsized celebrity, the real Leo began to disappear behind the one that was feverishly embellished by the media. It became difficult and then downright impossible to separate the truth from the growing legend.

Earlier on, Leonardo and his media advisors tried to counter every outlandish concocted tale with their version of "what really happened," but the denials came so thick and fast and painted Leonardo as a cross between Sir Lancelot and St. Francis, that they only contributed to the confusion. Leonardo finally withdrew, allowing the vultures to feed and making only such public appearances as he felt were necessary to promote his films or his own deeply felt convictions, such as the environment.

But even through unending hits on the Internet, the breathless image created by his multitude of fans and the towering mounds of suspect publicity, a picture of the man and the artist appears. As director for *Romeo + Juliet,* Baz Luhrmann pointed out, "The Leonardo DiCaprio I know is not the Leonardo I read about in the magazines."

On a personal note, he seems to have preserved much of the ingenuousness and likeability that marked his early years. He is courteous and polite. He is loved by his family and valued

by his friends, and he seems to have maintained that very real relationship throughout a career, where as a very young man, he has been subjected to the kind of pressures that have destroyed many others.

He sometimes lets his youthful exuberance get the best of him. Although the posse has been an anchor for him in times when his life threatens to become unmoored, he plays to his own gallery while pointedly ignoring the people or situations around him.

But perhaps the "real" Leo can be found in the words of others:

Carman Diaz: "He's a happy boy."

Claire Danes: "He's seen as this brash, impulsive, hot dude, which he is. But he's also, you know, tender."

Diane Keaton: "He's astonishing. He's a light."

Claire Danes (on first meeting him for *Romeo + Juliet*): "I found him quite geeky. But an entertaining geek."

Gretchen Moll (who played Leo's abused girlfriend in Woody Allen's *Celebrity*): "In Leonardo I saw someone who really isn't going to change his life and his lifestyle on how they might be perceived or something. I could tell that he was very loyal to his friends and that's what he's about."

Ioan Grufudd (Officer Lowe in *Titanic* and Lancelot in *King Arthur*): "Leonardo looks good when he's just hanging out, even in jeans and a t-shirt. He carries it off very elegantly, but he's tall, and he looks a lot more handsome in the flesh."

Jennifer Garner (who played a foxy hooker in *Catch Me If You Can*): "He's a movie star because he's such a good actor."

I could find no comment anywhere from any of Leonardo's friends and acquaintances that makes anything but the most complimentary assertions about the "Leo experience."

Professionally, the actor has also impressed his co-workers. Like any performer, he has known his share of bad reviews, but the experience of working with him has always generated a positive buzz.

Martin Scorsese: "When you look over his entire body of work, you see his power."

Russell Crowe: "It's beyond his being smart. He goes from strength to strength as an actor."

Tom Hanks: "Leo is so far ahead of the game. He's an incredibly talented guy who's been through ringers I can't even begin to comprehend. He's got nothing to learn from me.

Sharon Stone (on her impressions during *The Quick and the Dead* when Leo was 19): "Leo is a genius professionally and personally to a degree that is inspirational and frightening."

Steven Spielberg: "Leo is a very inventive actor with lots of ideas. He is also his own best critic. There were times [in the shooting of *Catch Me If You Can*] I'd accept a certain take, and Leo would say, 'No. No. I think there's something I haven't found yet. Let me do it again.' And he invariably came up with something that was just brilliant."

Agnieszka Holland (director of *Total Eclipse*): "He's a deeply interesting young man with a lot of integrity. He is certainly one of the most talented young actors I've ever worked with. He can still surprise us a lot of the time."

And Leonardo is determined that his "good time Charlie" image not tarnish his efforts to champion the environment. He is especially proud of being named Celebrity Chairman of Earth Day in 2000. The star made many appearances, taking full advantage of the profile the position gave him, and he wrote articles under such titles

> "Leo is a genius professionally and personally to a degree that is inspirational and frightening."

as "Get Wise to Global Warming." He also scored an interview (later broadcast on ABC) on the subject with then president Bill Clinton. The full text of their talk, published on the Internet, shows a well-prepared, articulate and intelligent Leonardo. The interview drove the media into a frenzy with ABC News star Sam Donaldson fuming, "[The stunt] Hollywoodizes the most serious of subjects." (As if somehow, Donaldson was anointed by some news god to be the only one who could conduct a cogent interview with the president. It's hard to imagine the doughty Donaldson pulling in the thousands of hits on the Internet that DiCaprio's chat with the president produced.)

Leonardo is known to be frugal. So much so that he frequently denies it in interviews, pointing out that he loves to drive expensive new cars or that he has bought his mother a new home. But the fact is, waitresses all over the world do not welcome his arrival. He is notorious for his under-tipping or not tipping at all. Many bars and clubs never send a bill over anyway; they are just happy to have so famous a movie star frequent their establishments. Leonardo and his pals often arrive, consume great quantities of booze and then just leave. But his financial attitudes no doubt were formed in his youth when his family lived on the edge of poverty. "I don't want to sound like some underprivileged kid," young Leo once told an interviewer, "but you learn certain values. Like not accepting that because you're in a hotel you have to pay $5.00 for a Coke. Just go down the block for a $3.00 six-pack." (Although it's a stretch to imagine Leonardo DiCaprio wandering down to the local 7-Eleven to pick up a six-pack of Coke.) "The best part of having money is not having to worry about it," says Leo. "We were very poor when I was a kid, and money was always on my mind."

> ...waitresses all over the world do not welcome his arrival. He is notorious for his under-tipping or not tipping at all.

For the record, he is known as a procrastinator; he twists his hair while thinking; he has a giggle that rasps on some people; and he smokes. He also bites his nails.

LEO FAN FACT

Despite his reputation as a lady-killer, Leonardo was once dumped by one of his high-profile, long-time girlfriends. Model Kristen Zang walked out on Leo just before he left for Thailand, stating that she was tired of "waiting for him to grow up."

Although he fronts an active production company, Leonardo shows little interest in writing or directing. He says, "Acting is enough for now. More than anything I want to travel. And I know I want to fall in love eventually."

Love? Not for the moment for the restless young star. "I don't know about getting married," he has said. "I'm probably not going to get married unless I live with someone for 10 or 20 years." Leo is obviously in no hurry. In September 2004, statuesque Brazilian supermodel Gisele Bundchen dumped the restless actor with the now-familiar comment quoted by a friend, "She is fed up waiting for him to pop the question." The two had been living together off and on for some time, which didn't seem to put much of a crimp in Leo's international romantic escapades. Said Gisele in the October 2004 issue of *Vanity Fair*, "This was the first love of my life. But it's been four years, and it's been hard. I've had to cancel a lot of jobs." Bundchen left two horses and three dogs to keep Leo company.

As he moves into his 30s, Leonardo has put a good deal of the Leomania of *Titanic* behind him. He now admits he was pulled in two ways by the experience. He indulged in the high life his celebrity offered while coming to loathe himself for what he was turning into. He had become the kind of person he didn't like—a little too famous, too rich, too pampered. For too long he was the epitome of the bed-hopping, hormone- and booze-fueled

Hollywood pretty boy. When the "pussy posse" was at its height, Leonardo fanned the flames by making highly visible appearances on the club scene almost every night. "When you're my age and your hormones are kicking in, there's not much else on your mind," he told an interviewer in an unguarded moment.

It all came to an abrupt end when one of Leo's closest friends, investment advisor Dana Giacchetto, was arrested and charged with stealing millions of dollars from Leonardo, Alanis Morissette and other high flyers. While using his lavish Manhattan pad as party central, the sham investor was powering his lifestyle with his friends' money. "That's the other side of fame," DiCaprio acknowledged to the *Sunday Times*. "Questioning people's intentions around you. Questioning how people came into your life. With me now," observes the chastened star, "people are guilty until proven innocent; before it was the other way around. I went into it blindly, not knowing I was being used by some people or who I should become involved with. It was pretty difficult for me and pretty overwhelming, and I certainly had a lot of people come into my life who were…less than favorable." In a somewhat rote quote, Leonardo went on ruefully, "I have a whole new set of rules and standards on women coming into my life. To know whether they are interested in me just because of who I am."

> **Leonardo has cut away the hangers-on and publicity seekers. He says that he now has about 10 close friends he spends his time with, mainly the gang he has known for a decade or more. You can still find his name in the columns nowadays, but mostly he parties in his lavish Hollywood Hills home. If anything, his experiences have driven him closer to his family. His mother and his father are still very much a part of his life.**

Flying in the face of the many stories to the contrary, Leonardo has always maintained that he never took drugs. Growing up on the mean streets of Los Angeles, he saw drugs ruin lives, and as a child, decided he would never embark on that dark road. He was also haunted by the tragic death of River Phoenix. "I choose not to do drugs," he says simply. He maintains that one of the reasons he made *The Basketball Diaries* was as a cautionary tale. Unfortunately, Leonardo performed the role of the heroin-addicted Jim Carroll so strongly in the film that, adding to his audience's tendency to see the actor as the parts he plays, reports of his drug use have circulated for years. It's hard to imagine that he could have achieved the quality of work and the number of movies that have distinguished his career if drugs had played much of a part in his life.

> Leo has said, "Don't think for a moment that I'm really like any of the characters I play. That's why it's called 'acting'."

Leonardo continues to fret over each role he takes. His father, his agents, advisors and lawyers all have input, but Leonardo makes sure the final decision is his. He scans each script carefully and ensures his co-stars are of a certain stature. "I'm not saying I'm above the rest or that I'll only work with big stars, but I do have guidelines. There are so many young actors who have gotten good roles at my age and later their careers slowly sloped down. Meaning no disrespect for anyone, but I don't want that to happen to me." In his choice of roles, he is always aware of making sure the momentum of his career will not spin away. It is important to him that he maintain the performance bar he set in his early films. He observes simply, "I've set a standard for myself, and hope I don't sell out and make stupid stuff."

Future projects remain uncertain. Every time Leonardo nibbles at a role, the media leaps on the story. The gossip columns even had him as Darth Vader a few years ago. His next film after *The Aviator* was to have been Baz Luhrmann's big-budget *Alexander the Great*, but the film has been delayed so much that its future is in question. Oliver Stone also has an equally ambitious version of the life of the bisexual conqueror of the ancient world starring Colin Farrell, and recent audience signs of turning away from *Gladiator*-type sword-and-sandal epics may keep it from the cameras. Years ago, Leonardo was rumored to be in line for the role of Sonny Corleone in a new Godfather film, and Leonardo's production company has shown interest in several properties including one on the life of surfer/con artist Miko Dora. He has also committed to Robert De Niro to star in *The Good Shepherd*, a historical film about the CIA.

It will come as no surprise to anyone reading this book that Leonardo wants to make sure he keeps his special relationships strong despite the demands on him personally and professionally. "The main thing for me is just to maintain my life with my family and friends. They treat me like 'Leo,' not 'Leonardo: Master Thespian.' That's all I need to maintain my sanity. I have just had to accept that being this famous is now part of who I am, and I have to incorporate that. Once I accepted that, I became more comfortable with it. But it took me a long time to figure it out."

The diversity of his film roles and the way he breathes life into them puts him in a special category of actor. He seems to have a sensitivity and emotional presence that allows filmgoers of all ages to access him on many different levels. As he enters the fourth decade of his life, the maturing Leonardo has become considerably more sanguine

> "I've come to realize that, no matter what happens, your work speaks for itself in the end. Once you realize that, nothing really matters. Even some of the lies make your life more interesting in the end."

about celebrity. "Post-*Titanic* was a pretty empty experience for me," he admits in the clarity of hindsight. "Being in the public eye and having the media define me as a certain thing. I hadn't really had any education in Hollywood. I was just a young man trying to figure things out. You know, for most things, you can go to a bookstore and read up about it. There is no book on how to deal with success, with the public's perception, what to do and what not to do. You know, I've come to realize that, no matter what happens, your work speaks for itself in the end. Once you realize that, nothing really matters. Even some of the lies make your life more interesting in the end."

LEONARDO DICAPRIO FILMOGRAPHY

Untitled Alexander the Great Project (2006)

The Departed (2006)

The Aviator (2004)

Catch Me If You Can (2002)

Gangs of New York (2002)

Don's Plum (2001)

The Beach (2000)

Celebrity (1998)

The Man in the Iron Mask (1998)

Titanic (1997)

Marvin's Room (1996)

Romeo + Juliet (1996)

Total Eclipse (1995)

The Basketball Diaries (1995)

The Quick and the Dead (1995)

Les Cent et une nuits de Simon Cinéma (1995)

The Foot Shooting Party (1994)

What's Eating Gilbert Grape (1993)

This Boy's Life (1993)

Poison Ivy (1992)

Growing Pains (1991–92) TV Series

Santa Barbara (1990) TV Series

Parenthood (1990) TV Series

Notes on Sources

Many of the quotes and some of the information in this book come from film specific interviews conducted by the author with Leonardo DiCaprio, Johnny Depp, Lasse Hallström, Juliette Lewis, Baz Lurhmann, Harold Perrineau, Diane Keaton, Meryl Streep, Claire Danes, Steven Spielberg, Tom Hanks, Martin Scorsese, Daniel Day-Lewis and James Cameron.

Other sources include (but are not limited to):

Bego, Mark. *Leonardo DiCaprio: Romantic Hero*. Kansas City: Andrews McMeel Publishing, 1998.

Looseleaf, Victoria. *Leonardo: Up Close and Personal*. New York: Ballantine Books, 1998.

Stauffer, Stacey. *Leonardo DiCaprio*. Philadelphia: Chelsea House Publishers, 1999.

McCracken, Kristin. *Leonardo DiCaprio*. New York: High Interest Books, 2000.

Catalano, Grace. *Leonardo: A Scrapbook in Words and Pictures*. New York: Bantam Doubleday Dell Publishing Group, 1998.

Degnen, Lisa. *Leonardo*. New York: Friedman\Fairfax Publishers, 1998.

Marsh, Ed W. *James's Cameron's Titanic*. New York: Harper-Perennial, 1997.

Scorsese, Martin. *Martin Scorsese's Gangs of New York*. New York: Miramax Books, 2002.

Colin MacLean

Colin Maclean began his career as a child actor in New Brunswick nearly half a century ago. Since then he has worked in just about every aspect of broadcasting, with regular duties on radio and television. During his two decades as an arts reporter for *Canada Now* and *CBC News*, Colin's film reviews and celebrity interviews were syndicated to television stations all over the country. He has spoken with some of the top names in show business and is now turning his experiences into star biographies.

ICON PRESS

STAR BIOGRAPHIES

Real stars. Real people. The life stories of show business celebrities.

JOHNNY DEPP; THE PASSIONATE REBEL
by Stone Wallace

Uncovers the real man behind the media hype. Is Depp really the "bad boy" he's made out to be by the paparazzi or simply a sensitive man who likes to keep his private life private. Colleagues describe Depp as a contemporary James Dean. He's certainly one of the most eclectic and eccentric actors ever to reach the heights of super stardom. A sexy, quirky actor, Depp chooses his roles on his own terms.

$7.95 USD/$9.95 CDN • ISBN 1-894864-17-4 • 5.25" x 8.25" • 144 pages

ORLANDO BLOOM
by Peter Boer

Hard to believe now perhaps, but when British actor Orlando Bloom appeared on the silver screen as Legolas in the first of the three *Lord of the Rings* films, he was a virtual unknown in the movie industry. In this readable biography, author Peter Boer details Bloom's rise to success, starting with his humble beginnings as a clay trapper at a Canterbury gun club. The book chronicles Bloom's progress through acting schools in London, as well as the back-breaking accident that changed the course of his life and propelled him on the path to stardom.

$7.95 USD/$9.95 CDN • ISBN 1-894864-18-2 • 5.25" x 8.25" • 144 pages

GWYNETH PALTROW
by Glenn Tkach

The daughter of producer Bruce Paltrow and actress Blythe Danner, Gwyneth Paltrow first stepped into the media's white-hot glare during her high-profile relationship with Hollywood hunk Brad Pitt. Now an Oscar winner, a mother, a fashion cover girl and an acclaimed stage actress, Gwyneth Paltrow has managed to fly under the radar of the media and remain an enigmatic and intriguing personality.

$7.95 USD/$9.95 CDN • ISBN 1-894864-24-7 • 5.25" x 8.25" • 144 pages

RUSSELL CROWE
by Stone Wallace

Russell Crowe has displayed a versatility applauded by audiences and critics alike, from his notorious early role as the brutal skinhead Hando in *Romper Stomper* to his astounding portrayal as the brilliant but schizophrenic math genius John Nash in *A Beautiful Mind*. Crowe has been compared to many of the great stars of yesterday: Marlon Brando, James Dean, even Robert Mitchum and Spencer Tracy. As this highly readable biography shows, however, Crowe is very much his own man—onscreen and off.

$7.95 USD/$9.95 CDN • ISBN 1-894864-19-0 • 5.25" x 8.25" • 144 pages

Look for books in the *Star Biographies* series at your local bookseller and newsstand or contact the distributor, Lone Pine Publishing, directly. In the U.S. call 1-800-518-3541. In Canada, call 1-800-661-9017.